# How to Succeed on a Majority Campus

## A Guide for Minority Students

Marc Levey
Michael Blanco
W. Terrell Jones
*Pennsylvania State University*

**Wadsworth Publishing Company**
I(T)P®    An International Thomson Publishing Company

Belmont, CA • Albany, NY • Bonn • Boston • Cincinnati • Detroit • Johannesburg • London • Madrid
Melbourne • Mexico City • New York • Paris • Singapore • Tokyo • Toronto • Washington

Publisher: Karen J. Allanson
Development Editor: Heather Dutton
Assistant Editor: Ryan Vesely
Marketing Manager: Chaun Hightower
Production Coordinator: Debby Kramer
Print Buyer: Barbara Britton
Permissions Editor: Peggy Meehan
Production: Vicki Moran/Publishing Support Services
Copy Editor: Elizabeth von Radics
Illustrator: Carl Yoshihara
Photographer: Marc Levey
Text Design: Vicki Moran
Cover Design: Seventeenth Street Studios
Compositor: Publishing Support Services
Printer: Edwards Brothers/Ann Arbor
Cover Printer: Phoenix Color Corp.

Printed in the United States of America
1  2  3  4  5  6  7  8  9  10

For more information, contact Wadsworth Publishing Company, 10 Davis Drive, Belmont, CA 94002,
or electronically at http://www.thomson.com/wadsworth.html

International Thomson Publishing Europe
Berkshire House 168-173
High Holborn
London, WC1V 7AA, England

International Thomson Editores
Campos Eliseos 385, Piso 7
Col. Polanco
11560 México D.F. México

Thomas Nelson Australia
102 Dodds Street
South Melbourne 3205
Victoria, Australia

International Thomson Publishing Asia
221 Henderson Road
#05-10 Henderson Building
Singapore 0315

Nelson Canada
1120 Birchmount Road
Scarborough, Ontario
Canada M1K 5G4

International Thomson Publishing Japan
Hirakawacho Kyowa Building, 3F
2-2-1 Hirakawacho
Chiyoda-ku, Tokyo 102, Japan

International Thomson Publishing GmbH
Königswinterer Strasse 418
53227 Bonn, Germany

International Thomson Publishing Southern Africa
Building 18, Constantia Park
240 Old Pretoria Road
Halfway House, 1685 South Africa

**Library of Congress Cataloging-in-Publication Data**

Levey, Marc.
How to succeed on a majority campus : a guide for minority
students / Marc Levey, Michael Blanco, W. Terrell Jones.
p.  cm.
ISBN 0-534-50671-2 (college). — ISBN 0-534-50672-0 (trade)
1. College student orientation—United States. 2. Minority
college students—United States. 3. Minorities—Education (Higher)—
United States. I. Blanco, Michael. II. Jones, W. Terrell. III. Title.
LB2343.32.L49   1998
378.1'9829'073—dc21
97-26358

# Contents

# Preface

# Reading This Book—What's in It for You?

An important question most readers ask themselves as they begin reading a book is *Why bother? What specifically can this book do for me?* In the case of the book you're holding right now, the answer is simple: help you grow. This book offers you a potpourri of thinking about the subject of minority students at majority campuses: It is part survival guide, part primer on college life, part historical review of relevant trends, part amalgam of student perspectives. We wrote this book not simply as a platform from which to give students advice, but as a way to explore ideas, open minds, and excite imagination. We wrote this book not just for prospective college students, but for their parents as well.

What you will find herein are both thematic and specialized chapters. Clearly, students will be interested in chapters on thematic issues such as "Relationships in College," "Ethics and Moral Decision Making," and "How to Put Skills into Your Studying," but we also urge you to peruse more-specialized chapters, such as "College and Asian American Women," "Lesbian, Gay, and Bisexual Students of Color," and especially the chapter written for your parents: "Helping Your Child Thrive in College: A Parent's Guide."

One of the challenges and strengths of this book is that it celebrates diversity and promotes empathy. Our goal is not to divide or trivialize through labels, but to explore the richness and variety that minority students have to offer their campuses. The final chapters of the book include excerpts from scores of minority student interviews—their personal histories, cultural heritage, and the impact of high school and college on their lives are individual and profound. We urge you to read this book as it was written—with open minds and hearts, with empathy and imagination.

This book is different for yet another reason. Over the course of the past ten years or so, a number of books have emerged on the general topic of "how to succeed in college." Although these books are broad-based guides to college success, some authors have realized that it is impossible to be all things to all people. Accordingly, more narrowly defined, specialized books on college success are now appearing, including books that stress important skills for college such as critical thinking, or even books aimed at a highly specific audience such as students who lack confidence. Prior to our book, however, very few, if any, publications have attempted to focus on the special needs of students of color attending predominantly white institutions (PWIs). It is clear that these students confront the same adjustment issues that white students do; however, they also face additional barriers associated with race, ethnicity, and cultural isolation. These barriers, which more generalized success manuals do not adequately address, are the focus of this book. We believe that there is compelling evidence that these obstacles are often the primary reasons some students of color might not succeed at PWIs, and our book is an attempt to place, in one volume, ideas and strategies that our joint experience and expertise suggest are most important for success in college.

## How We Dealt with the Problem of Terminology

From the outset, the authors of this book struggled with the issue of terminology. How should we refer to the audience and subject matter for this book? For some people, the very term *minority*—although commonly accepted in most contexts—implies a status that is pejorative and degrading. Clearly, we did not want to risk insulting the very audience we wish to reach.

Further, how should we refer, for instance, to individuals or groups of people who are of African descent? Are the terms *African American* and *Black* appropriate and acceptable? To whites probably yes; to numbers of non-whites, not necessarily.

You will understand the struggle the authors had in choosing terminology that is familiar and acceptable both to us and to you, our readers. In the end we chose to favor those terms most commonly accepted. Hence, this book mirrors society, which has not yet been fully successful in referring to minorities with uniform terminology that pleases everyone. This fact that we, as a society, cannot agree on racial and ethnic terminology provides us with just a hint of the complex nature of race in contemporary America. Given the scope and content of this book, however, it should be abundantly clear that the authors reject stereotypes, value individuality, and promote understanding.

As you read through the book, you might be tempted to feel at times that there are just too many obstacles to overcome at a predominantly white institution. Why put yourself through all this grief? We could tell you that adversity builds character, and this might be so. But it can also be draining and deflect one from the primary task at hand— to learn and grow personally and intellectually. We could also tell you that predominantly white institutions are good training grounds for the "real world," dominated as it is by white males. This might also be

At some schools you may feel isolated as in this image, which one of my students titled "One of these things is not like the others."

true, but an excellent education can be had at historically black colleges and other schools that are not predominantly white institutions.

We found a telling and common thread as we talked with scores of minority students who graduated from predominantly white institutions: The thread that binds is the belief that *Because I did well here, I am equipped to do well out there.* Ninety percent of the non-white graduates we surveyed stated that they would make the same decision to attend a predominantly white institution if they had to do it over again, and this was in spite of the fact that more than 75 percent of these same graduates reported having been subjected to or personally witnessed some form of discrimination in their years as undergraduates.

The bottom line is that your attendance at a predominantly white institution is probably going to mirror the state of society in general. And even though life for any college student poses a challenge, it can nevertheless be a richly rewarding experience. It is the aim of this book to help you make it so. We urge you to use the struggle and triumph of your brothers and sisters as a motivator. We believe you can do more than cope and struggle—you can win.

# Special Features

This book contains a number of special features that make it useful for students and parents alike.

- **Discusses the Merits of Non-Majority Institutions** The discussions throughout include the pros and cons of attending a majority institution versus historically or newly emerging institutions with greater than 50 percent minority student population.

- **Stresses Thriving, Not Merely Surviving** First and foremost, our experience with minority students tells us that students want more than to merely survive their college experience. We are convinced that students want their undergraduate careers to be marked by successes, both academically and socially.

- **Presents Student Experiences** This book presents the minority student experience from many viewpoints—from the students themselves as well as from counselors and other advisers who have worked with them extensively.

- **Includes a Chapter Written Specifically for Your Parents or Guardians** Chapter 2 contains information important not only to your parents or guardians but to you as well. The authors have tried to address the many questions parents commonly ask.

- **Tone Is Unvarnished** The authors have taken great pains to examine both the pluses and minuses of attending a predominantly white institution.

- **Gives Special Attention to Gender Issues** Chapters 7 and 8 are devoted to issues of particular concern to women of color.

- **Issues of Concern to Minority Gay, Lesbian, and Bisexual Students** Chapter 10 is devoted to specific issues faced by gay, lesbian, or bisexual minority students attending PWIs.

- **Discusses Extensively the Problems of Adjustment and Life** Key issues in contemporary living are addressed in individual chapters on moral and ethical decision making, relationships, and minority health.

- **Presents Feelings of Students** Because the decision to attend a PWI is often a highly emotional one, we have allowed those feelings to surface throughout the book. There has been no attempt to sanitize the text.

• **Includes the Stories of Students**   The book closes with two full chapters detailing interviews conducted with nearly a hundred American and international students of color attending PWIs across the United States. We believe that testimony can be a powerful learning vehicle. You will, therefore, find numerous personal statements from students in various chapters.

• **Special Pre-College Edition**   This edition contains material written especially for those of you actively considering college. The text is crammed with information that you and your parents need to make the right decisions before you enroll.

• **Contact with the Authors**   Finally, the authors invite you to share your critique, comments, opinions, and suggestions with us. Address your correspondence to:

C/O Marc Levey
308 Grange Building
Pennsylvania State University
University Park, PA 16802

Fax: (814) 863-2294

mbl1@psu.edu

## Acknowledgments

The authors wish to thank the many individuals who shared their ideas and comments with us in the writing of this book. In particular, we wish to offer our sincere thanks to all the students, past and present, who shared freely their frustration, anger, and joy during our many hours of interviews.

As a group, the authors wish to acknowledge the superior editing work done by Joe Schall, who in the process of bringing cohesion to the many writing styles became, in addition, one of the book's authors. To Gary Carlson of Wadsworth, our gratitude for sticking with the project and pushing us in the right direction. Also to Ryan Vesely from Wadsworth, our appreciation for his indulgence and patience. Finally, we wish to offer thanks to Geise Ly, who contributed photographs, read much of the manuscript, and offered encouragement and perception.

# Chapter 1

# Choosing the Right College for You

**W. Terrell Jones**

*When choosing a college or university, you must
consider the cultural fit between you and the school.*
—W. TERRELL JONES

Congratulations. You have worked hard and now you're ready to begin thinking about what college or university you will attend. As a young adult, you are involved in one of your life's most important choices—one that you must carefully research and use good judgment in making. Finding the correct fit between you and the school you choose could mean the difference between failure or success later in life.

Historically, a college education was a luxury for a very few. Those lucky enough to obtain a college degree were guaranteed professional and financial success. In 1900 only 4 percent of high school graduates attended college; but by the 1980s, more than 60 percent of high school graduates were going on to college. Given the realities of today's technologies and the information explosion, post-high school education is essential to ensure the best employment opportunities.

In continuing your education, you must choose from among many institutions of higher education, all of which vary in cost, size, location, admission standards, and educational philosophy. The financial expense of a higher education is always an important factor in deciding which school to attend. Schools range from large multicampus universities to small intimate colleges. As a potential student, you will have to choose what size institution best fits your needs, abilities, and temperament. Higher-education institutions also run the gamut of locations, from urban to suburban to totally rural settings. Finally, from an admissions point of view, some schools are selective, with academic requirements and prerequisites that fit only the most academically talented students. Other schools have admissions policies that are open to a greater number of students from a broader range within the academic spectrum.

All of these factors are critical variables that students must ponder, but as a student of color you must also consider the institution's cultural fit. What does this mean? In its simplest form, the concept of *cultural fit* asks you to consider whether there is a match between the institution's mission and your needs for community and cultural inclusion within the school of your choice.

It is not uncommon for students of color to think that they shouldn't have to consider cultural fit. They think that issues like cultural fit and race relations are relics of the past not relevant to their college experience. These students argue that institutions of higher learning are the last place one would expect to encounter racism, and that they have already been successful in communicating and making friends from a wide variety of cultural backgrounds. It is a fact, however, that in recent years institutions of higher education have experienced marked increases in acts of intolerance and both racial and cultural bias. These acts range from overt student confrontations to a more subtle institutional failure to recognize multicultural education issues.

One of our society's most cherished myths is that America's institutions of higher education are free of the turbulence and hostility of the real world, that they embrace and exemplify democratic ideals. Many students find that this is not the case, however. Despite the wealth of people, resources, and knowledge that institutions of higher learning have to offer, many students find that college campuses are places where social inequities are intensified, where competition for scarce resources brings out the worst in people.

All of these issues underscore the need for students of color to make an informed decision when selecting a college or university. Knowing what you want from higher education will assist you in making a more informed choice. Most important, an African American student must choose whether to attend a historically Black institution or a predominantly white institution.

## Historically Black Institutions

The genesis of *historically Black institutions (HBIs)* is directly tied to the American institution of slavery. Not until 1865, at the end of the Civil War, was a large-scale effort organized to educate freed slaves. The very first HBIs were, of course, located in the North and were established by the same Christian missionary movement that spawned the establishment of two hundred schools in America. Because a large number of these schools were organized without much long-term planning and with limited financial support, many were closed by 1900. Those HBIs that were fortunate enough to gain private, federal, or state financial support, however, were able to survive.

Today's HBIs have a long history of providing educational opportunities to African Americans. Many of our country's most respected and recognized African American leaders in civil rights, education, law, medicine, and business are graduates of HBIs. In 1950, 90 percent of all African American college students were enrolled in HBIs. Given the historically low levels of financial support, the fact that so many HBI students go on to hold national leadership roles is a testament to the dedication, quality, and success of HBIs.

Fleming (1984) and Mitchell (1993) suggest the following benefits to attending an HBI:

✔ Existence of a supportive community

✔ Ample opportunity for full participation

✔ Success in academic pursuits

✔ Strong opportunities for intellectual development

✔ The opportunity to interact on a daily basis with African American role models, both male and female, who are members of the faculty and administration

✔ The chance to network professionally with recent alumni and to follow in a long tradition of African American graduates of the school—a tradition that can't be found at most of America's predominantly white colleges

✔ Classes, whether in political science, sociology, history, English, or almost any other department, that incorporate Afro-centric themes

✔ Daily interaction with other motivated African American students

✔ A strong commitment to remedial programs in such areas as reading, writing, and math

✔ The ability to learn in an environment that is relatively free of racism and where the African American student is the center of attention

Although the above factors are strong incentives for choosing a historically Black institution, HBIs, like all types of schools, have drawbacks and may not be the best choice for all African American students. Chief among these drawbacks are the following:

✔ Limited opportunity to interact with a diverse student population

✔ Many HBIs are not well endowed financially, and it is difficult for them to update facilities and technologies

✔ HBIs tend to focus on teaching rather than research

✔ Test scores and high school preparation of students tend to be lower and of lesser quality, respectively, than for students who attend non-HBIs

In short, HBIs have many benefits but also include some disadvantages. The decision to attend a historically Black institution should be made carefully and with a great deal of introspection and self-assessment.

# Predominantly White Institutions (PWIs)

The migration of large numbers of African American students to *predominantly white institutions (PWIs)* began in the late 1950s. The civil rights movement and federal/state mandates persuaded PWIs to recruit African American students more aggressively. At present, approximately 75 percent of all African American students attend PWIs.

There are many factors that might influence an African American student to choose a PWI, including the following:

✔ Student body selectivity

✔ Perceived degree marketability

✔ Research opportunities

✔ Financial aid opportunities

✔ Academic reputation of school

✔ Advice from student support network

Although the reasons for attending PWIs are convincing, many African Americans have encountered serious problems while attending predominantly white institutions, some of which they were unaware even existed. African American students attending PWIs report such problems as:

✔ Difficulty adjusting to a predominantly white environment

✔ Racism, both subtle and overt

✔ Student self-segregation

✔ A perception of not being welcome, which in turn negatively affects what and how they learn

✔ Shortages of minority faculty/staff/graduate student role models and mentors

✔ Low levels of minority student retention

✔ Faculty insensitivity to African American students and multicultural issues

For PWIs, change is often difficult, even as they attempt to develop supportive campus climates for African American students. This difficulty arises chiefly because PWIs sometimes fail to recognize or understand the significant difference between equal and equitable treatment of African American students. Some PWIs assume that there are no real differences in the campus experience for African American students compared with white students; these schools tend to expect that minority students will easily assimilate into the larger student body without any difficulty. However well intentioned this one-size-fits-all philosophy may be, in reality the students who are culturally different from the white students pay a large price.

## Choosing Between an HBI and a PWI

As a prospective student debating the pros and cons of attending either an HBI or a PWI, the responsibility falls on you and your support network to research institutions and choose wisely based on facts. The old saying "caveat emptor" (let the buyer beware) should apply to your deliberations and final decision. You can begin thinking about that choice by better understanding your own needs and the expectations of your chosen institutions of higher education.

For those of you who are Hispanic, Asian American, or Native American, the options are not quite so clear-cut. Virtually all your choices will be limited to PWIs. With increasing participation of students of color in higher education, however, many campuses around the nation have become diversely populated with large numbers of Hispanic, Asian American, and Native American students. In several instances, former PWIs—for example, the University of California at Berkeley—are now *predominantly minority institutions (PMIs).*

No matter what your ethnicity, when considering whether or not to attend a predominantly white institution, you will need to address the following questions:

✔ What kind of student body do I want to be a part of?

✔ How does my high school student body compare and contrast with that of the institutions I am considering?

✔ How does the racial/cultural makeup of my home community compare with that of the schools I am considering?

✔ What kind of positive and negative interracial experiences have I had?

✔ What is the cultural makeup of the social groups to which I belong?

✔ Do I have good friends who are members of another racial or cultural group?

✔ What do I like to do for relaxation?

✔ How important is it for me to have African American or other minority faculty and staff role models?

✔ Do my friends or other members of my support network know anything about this school?

✔ How will graduating from this school assist me in achieving my career goals?

The answers to these questions are certainly not absolute determinants; however, reviewing them with parents, friends, and other members of your support network will help you make a choice that fits your goals.

## Choosing a School that Matches Your Cultural Fit

*Choosing a college is a lot like buying new jeans—you wouldn't pay good money for pants that don't fit; why should you pay to go to a school that does not fit your educational and social goals?*
—Freshman African American student

When assessing the cultural fit between yourself and a particular school, you must ask the right questions about the schools you are considering. Every college recruitment officer you meet has a positive attitude about the college he or she represents and is sincerely interested in having you attend that institution. After all, recruiting students is what college recruitment officers get paid to do. I am not suggesting that college recruiters are dishonest, but if you are to make the choice that is best for you, you need to be able to ask the right questions and know how to interpret the responses.

What follows are ten key questions, adapted from Mitchell (1993), that will assist you in assessing the cultural fit between yourself and the schools you are considering. Each question is followed by a set of potential answers and some ways of interpreting those answers. These questions will give you a strong feeling about the potential racial climate on campus, and the interpretations will help you understand the subtext that may be hidden beneath the answers.

1.  *What sort of academic and emotional support services does the school offer to African American (or other minority) students?*

    ✔ "We provide academic support for all students who request it."

    ✔ "Our students form study groups to provide their own academic support."

    ✔ "All of our students receive academic testing to assess deficiencies and are advised on what courses they should take."

    ✔ "We recruit only the best students and assume that they have the ability to be successful."

When considering the issue of academic and emotional support systems, look for some indication of the institution's sensitivity to your needs. Schools that realize that PWIs can have a disproportional negative impact on African American student success have services designed to address these issues.

2.  *How active and how large is the school's minority population?*

    ✔ "We treat all of our students the same; therefore, we have no need for exclusive student organizations."

    ✔ "We have a student-of-color advisory organization that meets the needs of all our minority students."

    ✔ "I think we have some, but they have not been very active over the past few years."

Look for minority support facilities. Their prominence on a campus can tell you a good deal about the racial climate.

> ✔ "Yes, our African American student organization is an active political and social student programming unit."

Look for some recognition that student organizations that support students of color are welcomed and supported by the institution. These organizations are useful in that they help African American students cope with a world that they can perceive as hostile and uninviting.

3. *What percentage of the campus population is African American, and what percentage of the campus population includes minorities other than African Americans?*

   > ✔ "Our percentages are low, but we are working on improving our numbers."

   > ✔ "In some colleges and departments, the percentages are good and in some they are very low."

   > ✔ "We have a very successful minority recruitment and retention program that strives to achieve numbers equal to the representation in the state."

✔ "We admit only students who are qualified for admission without regard to race or ethnicity."

In an attempt to appear inclusive, many schools develop recruitment brochures that give the impression that the actual number of African American students is large. Many times students who attend the schools feel cheated to learn that this is not the case.

4.   *What are the racial attitudes of the majority of the students at the school?*

✔ "All of our students appear to get along, and we see ourselves as one big happy family."

✔ "In the past we have had some very serious racial problems on campus that appear to be the work of outside agitators."

✔ "We provide programs for all of our students on understanding one another and promote the importance of cultural diversity."

✔ "We provide all entering African American students with an upper-class buddy who helps them adjust to our campus."

Schools that have a more open-minded or progressive student population tend to be more tolerant of racial and cultural diversity. Look to see if the institution is proactive in promoting positive cultural relations on campus. The day after an incident occurs is the worst time to develop tolerance.

5.   *How large and how integral a part of the curriculum is the school's Black Studies courses or program?*

✔ "We have some Black Studies elective courses that are very popular with our African American students."

✔ "There are no Black Studies courses in our curriculum."

✔ "Our school has a fully integrated curriculum, where all students are required to participate in multicultural education."

✔ "Our school provides a one-credit course in understanding one another that is part of the new freshman orientation program."

If you are African American and your ethnic and cultural heritage are important to you, you should consider schools where these facets of your college education can be enhanced. Also look for indicators that the entire curriculum has a multicultural focus.

6. *How quick is the administration when it comes to responding to incidents of racism on campus, and how effective and supportive is its response?*

   ✔ "In situations of racial bias or acts of intolerance, we move quickly to find out who is responsible, and they are referred to our office of conduct standards."

   ✔ "Like everybody else, we are struggling to deal with these issues and have not yet found the solution."

   ✔ "Our school is a place of higher education and enlightenment; we do not have those kind of problems."

   ✔ "We are in the process of reinventing our school. We are making our entire campus community confront the basic question of how to best prepare students to live in a radically changing world."

When considering the administration's response to potential racial incidents, look for some institutional recognition that they are working on this problem and that your concerns are valid.

7. *What are the graduation rates for both African American and majority students?*

   ✔ "I think that African Americans graduate at a rate similar to that of majority students."

   ✔ "Our goal is to have African Americans graduate at the same rate as our majority students, and we have made consistent progress toward that goal."

   ✔ "African Americans who work hard and apply themselves are graduating from our school."

   ✔ "My job is the recruitment of students, and I can tell you that those numbers are up. You will have to talk to someone else about graduation rates."

Try to find indicators that African American retention and graduation are important issues at the school. Be suspicious of a recruiter who is ignorant of graduation or retention rates.

8. *Have there been any major racial incidents at the institution in the past two years?*

   ✔ "We have had some major incidents involving issues of race, and they were handled to the satisfaction of all persons involved."

   ✔ "It has been our experience that the media blow these things out of proportion and that they inflate many of the problems."

   ✔ "We hire sensitive and caring faculty and staff, and they handle these situations."

   ✔ "These issues are reported to the office of multicultural affairs. You should talk with them about your concerns."

Although a school may not be able to control whether a racially motivated incident occurs, how it deals with such incidents is an indicator of its sophistication and ability to address future concerns.

9. *What percentage of the faculty and staff are African American, and what percentage are other minorities?*

   ✔ "We have had problems retaining African American faculty and staff."

   ✔ "Our administration has made increasing the number of African American faculty and staff a top priority for our school."

   ✔ "We hire only the best faculty and staff without regard to race or ethnicity."

   ✔ "We have African American faculty and staff in our Black Studies Department."

A school cannot be sincerely interested in African American students unless it is providing them with appropriate role models and mentors. These role models should not be involved simply in the Black Studies program; there must be a total institutional commitment.

10. *What was the academic profile of last year's entering African American and majority freshman class?*

   ✔ "We look for a well-rounded student who can do college-level work."

At some colleges with few minorities, students end up studying alone.

✔ "Don't worry about that—we are interested in you."
✔ "Most of the African American students in last year's class were competitive with the majority students in the class."
✔ "We don't expect African American students to have the same academic profile as majority students."

In their rush to increase African American and sometimes Hispanic student recruitment, some schools throw academic standards to the wind and admit almost any African American or Hispanic student who applies. However well intentioned this attempt may be, the results are predictable. Large numbers of students admitted under these conditions are usually not successful and would have been better served at an institution where their academic ability was similar to that of the rest of the student body.

## Conclusion

Clearly, the cultural fit between a minority student and his or her school of choice can be the most important variable in the success of that student. Higher-education institutions differ greatly in their sensitivity to issues facing African American and other minority students. When you choose a college, it is your future at stake and you must ask the right questions and receive the right answers if you want to make the best choice.

## References

Fleming, Jackie. *Blacks in College: A Comparative Study of Students' Success in Black and White Institutions* (San Francisco: Jossy-Bass, 1984).

Mitchell, Ralph. *The Multicultural Student's Guide to College* (New York: Noonday Press, 1993).

# Chapter 2

# Helping Your Child Thrive in College: A Parents' Guide

**Marc Levey**

This chapter will assist you in making informed decisions about how you may best help your son or daughter succeed in his or her post-secondary education. We know with near certainty that without either a technical or college education beyond high school, your child will find it exceedingly difficult to move ahead in the world of the twenty-first century. The problems facing both you and your child as he or she contemplates higher education are formidable indeed, but this is not to say that the problems are insurmountable—they aren't!

All of us want our children to do better than we did. We also have the luxury of hindsight: We look back and often wish we had made different decisions at various times in our lives. Sometimes we also wish our own parents had acted differently. Perhaps they should have involved themselves more in our decision making when we were young, or perhaps they should have left us alone more to make our own choices. However clear our hindsight or far-reaching our vision, there is no one right strategy guaranteed to produce positive outcomes for our children—we all have to play it as we see it. Even so, it is one thing to make blind choices and quite another to make decisions and offer support from an informed perspective.

You have probably realized that education is one of the principal keys to upward mobility in a society that is essentially two-tiered. And many non-whites, regardless of ability, can still find it difficult to progress at the same rate as their white peers. The sad truth is that a great many people do not mind a two-tiered society so long as they are in the upper tier. This is reflected in white America's lack of support for programs and policies, both public and private, aimed at redressing historic inequities that exist in our society.

For these and other reasons, it is more important than ever that our children receive training or education relevant to twenty-first-century challenges. Education is the only thing that will give many of our children a chance to prosper in a social environment that is increasingly competitive and divisive. Only those individuals with superior skills will be able to overcome the inequities of a "have/have not" system.

This chapter is divided into specific topics for you to consider. Overriding all of the information and suggestions is one mighty truth—the one thing you must do above all else, the one thing you must do in spite of evidence to the contrary: *You must be involved and you must be the cheerleader!* When things get rough—and they will—be positive. When grades are poor, offer encouragement. When your child seems miserable and lonely, listen. When he or she wants to quit, help find another solution. These are the most important things you can do. And they are by far more important than money or any other form of material assistance you provide.

Sometimes parents come to believe that they no longer matter once their children begin their post-secondary education. Nothing is farther from the truth! Our kids just need us in different ways. We need to learn new ways of supporting their aspirations. For most parents it's difficult to simply stand by and watch as their children make mistakes. This is another hard truth: When your kids leave home for school, you immediately lose a good deal of control. What appears at first to be a case of the children abandoning the family and its values for their newly found freedom, however, is not necessarily a permanent situation. So don't give up! Try to be patient and understand that what seems to be rejection is merely part of the rite of passage from semi-dependent adolescence to mostly independent young adulthood.

To ease your way into your new role as physically distant yet emotionally active supporters of a college student, this chapter is designed to address your questions and concerns. The material comes from discussions with actual parents of minority high school and first-year college students, and the students' counselors and advisers.

## The Parents' Role: Give Up Some Power, but Be Involved

You can be most helpful to your child if you assume the role of chief supporter and hypercheerleader. As the parent of several college-age children, I recognize the difficulty of shifting from the role of primary decision maker to that of active supporter. This is especially hard when it's your money that's financing your child's tuition and living expenses. Even if you don't choose to, however, circumstances will dictate a change in the parent/child power relationship. It's easier to just give up some of the power and control voluntarily, and such a move has the added benefit of demonstrating your trust and confidence in your son or daughter.

Before your child actually matriculates, he or she will need to make several decisions that should include your active involvement. The first step is sifting through all the possible career choice possibilities. There is a wide variation in how well school systems prepare students for making career choices, so don't automatically assume that your child's school does a competent job in this area, even if you believe the system is generally a good one.

Here are a few simple guidelines to consider as you assist your student with these important life decisions:

✔ Always consider your child's preferences first.

✔ If your sixteen year old says he or she wants to be a brain surgeon, support that aspiration and take it as far as it goes. In other words, don't automatically rule anything out.

✔ Help your student assess his or her skills and interests, then see how those interests match up with the stated career choice. Obviously, if your student wishes to be an engineer but has a history of difficulty with mathematics and science, you may wish to question the choice without absolutely ruling it out.

✔ Listen to your child's reasons for choosing a particular career or vocation. Consider how well thought out his decision is or whether it is just a whim. A good test of how serious he is about a particular career choice is to see how well he can describe what exactly one does in the chosen career. Usually, the more detailed and precise he is, the more serious you can assume he is about the choice.

✔ Try to resist the temptation to steer your student into popular or prestigious careers, particularly if he or she shows no interest. Understand that motivation is at least as important as ability when it comes to academic success.

✔ Have your student identify what she is good at and try to match those skills and talents to particular careers.

✔ With the help of school guidance counselors, have your student tested for vocational preferences. There are several standard inventories that will give general guidance. These batteries provide a good starting point and are especially useful for individuals who have no strong career preferences.

✔ Have your student consider all education, training, and work-experience options. Chief among these are: two-year and four-year colleges or universities; community colleges; proprietary schools (vocational, technical, or career-specific programs of various kinds); military training; and work experience.

✔ If your student has a definite preference at any point, have him talk with someone already in the field. If the preference is medicine, for instance, a talk with the family doctor could either strengthen or possibly weaken career interest in the field.

✔ Don't assume that certain careers are gender-specific. Both women and men can succeed at virtually any career.

✔ Perhaps most important, have your student do the lion's share of the work. Let her do the research. Take an active part only when you are asked, but stay involved as a sounding board.

When considering the preceding advice, keep in mind that many students select an academic major that does not match their interests and abilities or even prepare them in any way for their intended careers. Many students go to college simply to fill up the four years between high school and work, or because their parents think that getting a college degree is nonnegotiable. As a parent helping your child choose a potential career, you must juggle the roles of adviser, friend, and resource person, and you must do so in a way that your advice can be accepted without your taking over your son's or daughter's job.

# The Job Outlook for the Twenty-First Century

There are two sides to the career coin: On one side is your child's job options, and on the flip side is information about where employment will be in the twenty-first century. This is where reality comes into play. It's one thing to say, "I really want to be a small farmer," but it is quite another to confront reliable data indicating that the small farm, as we know it, will virtually cease to exist within the next twenty years. Should one press on and become a farmer in spite of this evidence? This is a difficult question to answer.

One resource we do have is a number of well-documented job forecasts, usually prepared by federal agencies. One such forecast that is often quoted is the United States Department of Labor's *The 1992–2005 Job Outlook in Brief*. This document outlines the major jobs and careers that will decline and those that will increase over the next fifteen years.

These predictions demonstrate that there are significant shifts in career prospects in store for us. But keep in mind that simply because a certain career is on the high-growth list, that doesn't make it an automatic winner for your son or daughter. Conversely, an occupation on the slow-growth list should not be ruled out completely. Share this list with your student and see if anything strikes a responsive note. You may also wish to encourage him or her to investigate computer-aided career search systems such as Discover or Sigi Plus.

The key thing to remember when helping your son or daughter consider a career is that adolescents are most influenced by their peers and may resist your efforts to impose your judgments on them. The watchword is "Easy does it." Patterns in post-secondary education are changing rapidly, with many students continuing their education later in life. Adult learners represent a larger percentage of the student population than ever. So, again, be patient.

## Ways to Introduce Your Child to Post-Secondary Education

One way to introduce your student to post-secondary education is through the many readiness programs offered to junior and senior high school minority students by large numbers of colleges and universities throughout the country. Some of these programs are federally funded under the Department of Education's Trio Programs umbrella. The best known of these is Upward Bound. Another is Special Student Services, or SSS. College admissions offices and career centers should be able to provide specific information about what's available in your area. Also, be aware that any number of these programs stress study skills and survival techniques as well as academic development.

This leads us to the next facet of your role as the parent of an aspiring college student. Success in post-secondary education is largely dependent on two things: a *positive attitude* and a *good work ethic*. If you begin encouraging your children early, they grow to believe in themselves. Each time they make even a modest improvement, reinforce it; you can't overpraise them. Along with reinforcing a positive "can do" attitude, try to help your son or daughter develop a good work ethic. Here are a few basic things you can do without seeming overly controlling:

✔ If possible, set aside a space where your student can study.

✔ Control other children's activities and noise during study time.

✔ Negotiate a reasonable study period, including an amount of time and number of days.

✔ Determine what a meaningful, reasonable incentive would be and offer it, not only for grades, but for the sustained effort to do the best job possible. To many students, the symbolism is as important as the material reward.

✔ When your children do something well in school, on the job, or in their personal activities such as hobbies or sports, *go public.* Let your kids know that you are proud of their achievements and that you want everyone to know. Sometimes your kids may feel embarrassed by the attention, but most of the time they'll be really pleased. The achievement does not always need to be something big; even modest improvement can be cause for celebration.

You can play a role in your child's selection of the most appropriate form of post-secondary education at about the same time the career search takes place. In the best of all possible worlds, the two are thought of concurrently, but it doesn't always work out that way. Many times the two decisions are made in a virtual vacuum, but, with your help, your student will grow to see them as intertwined.

## Types of Post-Secondary Education

Far too often we assume that the only choices for post-secondary education are among the various four-year colleges and universities. Not true! There are dozens of alternatives, from job-specific apprenticeships, vocational and proprietary schools offering short- to medium-length training, and community colleges featuring certificate and associate degree programs. Military training offers education that is on the cutting edge of technology and science. Many of these programs are flexible so that participants can work and still go to school. Do not rule out on-the-job training, either, particularly if your son or daughter doesn't seem ready for the rigors of post-secondary education.

The table on pp. 23–27 summarizes the main types of formal and informal education available today. Note that the annual costs shown are the total outlay, from all sources, to support one student for a single academic year, which is generally nine to ten months. These costs are approximate and include tuition, room and board, books and supplies, incidental expenses such as transportation, some medical costs, entertainment, and laundry. Many students find that they require even more than these estimated costs to get through an academic year.

## Factors to Consider When Choosing a College

There are many factors that you and your son or daughter should consider when choosing a college, including location, racial climate, finances and financial aid, housing, and, especially, academic program offerings.

### Location

For many parents the choice of which institution is right for their child comes down to location. For some students it is of utmost importance to get away from home and begin anew in fresh surroundings. That might mean matriculating at a campus in a rural setting, even though the student has always lived in the city. In addition to the tremendous adjustment of a new living situation, your son or daughter may also be facing adjustment to a whole new set of sounds, activity levels, and even style of dress and language patterns. The same holds true for students from rural or suburban communities who decide to matriculate at urban institutions.

Your son or daughter must weigh the advantages and disadvantages of any particular location. For some minority students, having access to a community they relate to and can find comfort in is very important. For others this is not a significant factor in choosing a school. It may be that security is a prime consideration; if it is, perhaps a school in a rural location is a wise choice.

What I am suggesting here is that the choice of a school's location is, by necessity, a compromise. You can help your son or daughter decide what demographic factors are most important—for example, large versus a small student body, or a rural versus an urban setting. And when it comes down to making a a final selection, only an actual

## Educational Institution Comparison

| Institution Type | Total Annual Cost | Advantages | Disadvantages |
|---|---|---|---|
| Four-year college, public, 10,000+ students | $7,500–12,000 | Almost unlimited selection of academic programs, many student services, possibility of a minority community, reasonable value for the money. | Course selection can be bewildering, atmosphere impersonal, tendency to "get lost." Many distractions. The student must be reasonably mature to deal with the pressure. |
| Four-year college, public, 5,000–10,000 students | $7,500–12,000 | Many of the same advantages as at larger institutions, plus a somewhat more personal approach. | Somewhat fewer course offerings than at larger schools. Schools could be less prestigious. |
| Four-year college, private, 5,000–20,000 students | $15,000–30,000 | Many offer high prestige, excellent facilities, top-notch academic programs, and first-rate faculty. Graduates are heavily recruited by industry and graduate schools. | An undergraduate education could cost as much as $125,000. Some question whether the cost matches the benefit. |

## Educational Institution Comparison, *continued*

| Institution Type | Total Annual Cost | Advantages | Disadvantages |
|---|---|---|---|
| Four-year college, private, 1,500–5,000 students | $15,000–30,000+ | Great variety, from smaller Ivy League institutions to very small denominational schools with specific church affiliations. Small schools offer personal attention at the expense of more limited program offerings and smaller faculties. Minority students may feel isolated because of small numbers. Some schools offer highly specialized courses of study such as art, engineering, and architecture. | Many of the same advantages as at the large private schools apply. Some smaller schools do not possess extensive lab facilities or large faculties. Many are located in small rural settings. |
| Community colleges, 1,000–20,000 students | Costs vary | Wide range of programs, from basic two-year college curriculum to vocational and technical course offerings. Varied and flexible course scheduling with | Very few upper-level courses in any one academic discipline. Students who begin at a community college must transfer if they wish to complete a |

| Institution Type | Total Annual Cost | Advantages | Disadvantages |
|---|---|---|---|
| | | both daytime and evening classes, allowing students to attend school while working. Student-centered faculty. Students can live at home and commute. Usually located centrally in urban or suburban areas. Greater access to minority communities. Many programs are on the cutting edge of technology because of industry involvement. Students incur less debt and begin their careers sooner than students at four-year colleges. These institutions often relate better to minority communities than more traditional colleges and universities. | baccalaureate program. Often the faculty are part-time and difficult to reach for consultation. Degrees from community colleges may not be as prestigious as those from an accredited four-year institution. |

## Educational Institution Comparison, *continued*

| Institution Type | Total Annual Cost | Advantages | Disadvantages |
|---|---|---|---|
| Proprietary schools | $1,500–10,000 | As at community colleges, there is a wide range among these institutions. Proprietary schools generally offer narrowly defined programs of study, usually specific to a career in fields such as cosmetology, broadcast technology, art, and business. Students can begin their careers rapidly. Many schools offer flexible payment plans, and some feature extensive job placement services. | Some programs sacrifice well-rounded curriculums in social sciences, behavioral sciences, and the like in order to concentrate on skill-specific academic courses. There are relatively few student support services. |

| Institution Type | Total Annual Cost | Advantages | Disadvantages |
|---|---|---|---|
| Military Training | Free | Some of the finest technical training available anywhere. Immediate employment usually in the same field. Constant updating and opportunities for further, more sophisticated education. Most military bases offer on-site college programs which are not free but are government subsidized. Promotions may come more rapidly than at other jobs. | Must commit to the military for a period of several years. May have little choice of job location. Many young people are not willing to accept the discipline and regimentation. |

on-site visit or two will give any accurate sense of the place. It's not scientific, but it's important that the campus feel "feel right." By the second visit, your student should get a positive feeling from the surroundings, even taking into account the natural tendency to feel a bit overwhelmed. And keep in mind that college admissions literature will put only the best face on a school; very rarely—if ever—will an institution admit to any sort of problems on its campus.

## Racial Climate

When you make a campus visit, it is unrealistic to expect the students you talk to, most of whom are carefully selected by school administrators, to give you a true sense of the racial climate of a campus. You'll need to dig a bit further.

A minority administrator friend of mine stated flatly that the only way to find out what's going on is to question students at random in the student union or other public place on campus. She also suggested that, in terms of racial balance, public places like the student union or dormitory dining hall should look like a typical first-grade classroom; that is, they should not look like the students are self-segregated. A reasonable mix of minority and majority students in these informal settings is a good indication that the campus climate is conducive to positive intergroup relations.

Another consideration in determining a school's racial climate is the number of senior tenured minority faculty and top administrators. Although progress has been made at many educational institutions in diversifying the faculty and administrators, there is still not a significant number of minorities in the top echelons. Most predominantly white institutions are still controlled by whites, and especially white males—a fact that will not surprise many readers.

Suffice it to say that the choice of location and the racial climate of a campus are at least of equal importance to any other factor in deciding on a college. But keep in mind that there are thousands of institutions from which to choose, and no one school is likely to be a perfect fit.

To help prepare for a multicultural living experience, you should begin by assessing your child's past social and educational experiences. What you say and do should be largely conditioned by your child's prior experiences with racism. If your child comes from a largely Black urban high school and neighborhood, for instance, his ability

Some students report that they feel more comfortable with an adviser or counselor of their own race than with one who is white.

to deal with the challenges of multicultural living may be quite different from those of another Black student who has lived and gone to school in a racially mixed suburban environment. For numbers of minority students used to growing up in an ethnic community, the initial experience of living on a predominantly white campus may very well be a form of culture shock.

At times, tensions and racial friction arise between new roommates, often exacerbated by the attitudes of their parents. You cannot do much to help here, other than rely on the school. Your child, the roommate, and the school will have to work these things out. You should know that many schools that provide dormitory space will not automatically move a student to another room because there appears to be a problem based on race or ethnicity. Instead, the residence hall staff will attempt to help the roommates work through the issues. It might be wise to inquire about policies governing these situations, even though they are relatively uncommon. The answer you get from school officials could be yet another indication of the racial climate on the campus.

## Finances and Financial Aid

A problem that all parents must solve is that of financing their children's education, and this is the subject that parents of minorities typically ask about the most. This section cannot answer all of your questions about finances and financial aid, but it does address some of the most typical concerns.

The following are some basics that all parents should know about finances and financial aid:

- ✔ Virtually all financial aid is based on need, which is calculated based on your family income.

- ✔ There are a few, although not many, aid sources that are not need-based, such as specific scholarships.

- ✔ Most financial aid is awarded on a first-come first-served basis, so apply as early as possible.

- ✔ To receive any student aid, most schools ask you to complete the Free Application of Federal Student Aid (FAFSA) by the date specified by the particular institution. Returning students usually need to file a renewal application each year. The FAFSA, in both English or Spanish, is available from high school guidance counselors and the financial aid offices of virtually any post-secondary educational institution.

- ✔ From the information you provide, most of which comes from your current federal income tax return, the institution's financial aid office will compute a need analysis. Based on this information, a "family contribution" is calculated. The family contribution, along with the predetermined cost of attendance, will determine your child's maximum eligibility for student aid.

- ✔ Three key terms to be aware of are *grant, scholarship,* and *loan.* The first two need not be repaid. Any financial aid labeled loan, however, must eventually be repaid, usually with interest added to the principal amount. Because of today's heavy budget cutting, most aid comes in the form of loans. These days it is not unusual for a graduating student to owe $15,000 in loans or perhaps much more.

- ✔ In our credit-oriented society, programs exist to repay these large loan amounts over periods of up to ten years.

✔ If your family income is in excess of $50,000 and you have two or fewer children, you probably will not be eligible for federal or most state grants. You may, however, be eligible for one or more of the loan programs set up to aid low- and middle-income families.

✔ A majority of students at post-secondary vocational and proprietary schools are eligible for federal and state aid, just as those at two- and four-year colleges and universities are.

✔ A number of institutions still offer financial aid earmarked for minority students. In view of recent Supreme Court decisions, it remains uncertain whether these sources will survive.

✔ Many schools, principally those with large endowments, offer attractive financial incentives to students who have excelled academically. If your student has done well in high school and has very high SAT scores, you should look into college scholars programs.

✔ Finding the best financial aid deal is a complex process. Do some comparison shopping, and don't have your son or daughter accept the first offer if others are outstanding.

✔ Other than loans that you take out as the parent, such as the Plus Loan, most loans incurred by students who are eighteen or older are their responsibility. In other words, your child and not you is responsible for the loan debt and subsequent repayment.

✔ Higher-education costs have been rising at a much faster rate than the general cost of living. Expect an annual increase of 4 to 7 percent in tuition, fees, and room and board.

✔ Financial aid can continue beyond the traditional four years. Institutions set policies for academic progress.

✔ For financial aid purposes, summer attendance usually doesn't count as a term or semester.

✔ The average college student spends four and a half years in college and changes academic majors at least once in that period. For most students there is no longer a traditional four-year college degree; it often takes longer, and the degrees often include specialization.

✔ Many courses of study automatically require five or more years to complete. Among these are architecture, several engineering majors, education programs requiring student teaching, and programs of study requiring a co-op position with industry or study abroad.

✔ If your son or daughter receives a financial aid package and it doesn't cover incidentals with a refund after tuition and fees, he or she will need an additional $20 to $30 per week for such expenses as over-the-counter medicine, entertainment, laundry, and personal hygiene items.

✔ Having your student live at home, with all its advantages and admitted disadvantages, will save about 30 percent of the overall cost of his or her education.

✔ Generally, it is better for students not to work during the first semester. If they must or really want to work, they should limit their work schedule to a maximum of about 15 hours per week.

✔ Almost all post-secondary institutions have a financial aid office. Financial aid officers are experts on the ins and outs of this complex subject and can answer just about any question you might have about applying for financial aid. They are often difficult to reach by phone and can be contacted more effectively by e-mail or a personal visit.

### Housing

One of the first decisions students need to make once they are accepted into a post-secondary institution is where they will live. Essentially, there are four choices:

1.   On-campus institutionally run housing
2.   Off-campus institutionally run housing
3.   Off-campus rental housing
4.   Home

Like every other decision related to college, each housing alternative offers pluses and minuses. You and your child must take this decision seriously, for it can make the difference between a supportive and a negative environment. This section examines each option in some detail.

**On- and Off-Campus, Institutionally Run Housing**   Usually in the form of residence-hall living, this type of arrangement offers the advantage of a safe, controlled environment and provides most of the essential facilities, such as for laundry, study, and nearby dining. It also includes computer terminals, many social and educational programs, and a trained live-in staff.

Schools usually offer the room with one of several meal plans (if dining facilities exist on campus) in a legally binding housing contract much like a lease. And though you may hear loud complaints about the quality or diversity of the food served in school dining halls, it is usually several notches above typical institutional food. Dining-hall meals are nutritionally balanced and abundant; there is usually a wide assortment of ethnic food on a regular basis, as well as typical all-American fare. Above all else, the food is readily available, of reasonable quality, and prepaid. In other words, there is no reason for your student to ever go hungry.

Residence-hall rooms themselves vary greatly, even on the same campus, but they generally come with essential furniture: a bed, mattress, desk, chair, lamp, and bureau or dresser/closet combination for each roommate. Some residence-hall setups provide private bathrooms, but most do not; standard is a gender-segregated common bathroom on each floor or in each suite.

A new trend in educational housing is the construction of cluster or garden-type apartment housing. In this arrangement two, three, or four or more students share what amounts to a small townhouse or apartment. Each unit can contain a communal kitchen, one or more full bathrooms, common living and working spaces, and private or semi-private bedrooms. Residential-life personnel are typically assigned to each group of units.

The drawbacks associated with residence-hall living for first-year students are relatively few. In fact, many institutions with on-campus residence halls make living in them mandatory for at least the first year, in part because it helps students adjust rapidly to college life along with their peers.

There are two possible disadvantages to living in the residence halls for the freshman year. First, some students may feel overly controlled with too many rules to follow. And just when they thought they were getting away from Mom and Dad's restrictions! Second, most room assignments are made randomly, except when two individuals request the same room early enough for the room assignment office to arrange it. In some cases, even requesting a specific roommate is no guarantee that it will happen.

**Off-Campus Rental Housing**   In most areas surrounding an educational institution, one can find a wide variety of rental housing, from high-rise multioccupant units to single rooms in private homes. The quality of these accommodations varies from excellent to downright awful. Some students put up with really dreadful housing even though they are paying as much as their peers who are living in much more comfortable digs. In any event, a great number of students find the prospect of living off campus very attractive. Some institutions do not provide any on-campus living facilities. In these instances your son or daughter has no choice but to find off-campus housing.

Before signing a rental agreement, there are several things you and your child should know. Most of the following information comes from a series of interviews with a university administrator who has spent many years researching and advising parents and students about renting housing.

- ✔ Any contract signed by your eighteen year old is legally binding *on him or her.*

- ✔ A relatively new phenomenon in rental housing is the application to rent. Some of these applications are used as simple screening devices, whereas others ask for a fee that is nonrefundable if a lease is not signed. Be careful that signing doesn't legally commit your student to a lease.

- ✔ If your child is under eighteen years old, a parent must sign and is therefore liable for all the conditions spelled out in the lease.

- ✔ Read the lease carefully, especially sections dealing with late fees, deposits, and property damage. Even the so-called plain language leases now required by many states warrant careful study.

- ✔ There are any number of different types of leases. They are called by different names around the country, but they usually fall into one of two categories: joint leases and individual leases. In a *joint lease,* your student is responsible for his or her part of the rent *and the roommates' rent* in the event that the roommate or roommates do not pay their portion of the rent. Each leasee is responsible for the entire rental contract, even if the other roommates move out or leave town. In an *individual lease,* your student is responsible for paying only his or her share of the rent, no matter what the other roommates do. Obviously, this type of lease is most advantageous to the renter.

✔ Be certain to read the lease carefully for extra fees—for late payment of rent, for subletting, for parking or pets, for repairs, and so on. If they are not in the lease, the tenant can't be charged for them.

✔ Before moving in, have your student check the apartment, house, or room and document its condition. Have your student take pictures, keep copies, and give the landlord a copy.

✔ For many landlords, renting is their business. Do not expect special treatment simply because of your child's status as a student.

✔ Expect that some apartment owners may make negative assumptions and comments about students, such as "They'll trash the place" or "They have no respect for my property." Be prepared to deal with such attitudes.

✔ Some landlords form stereotypes about ethnic or racial groups. This can and does lead to a certain amount of racism in renting. You could agree to everything on the telephone, but when you show up in person, the property is suddenly rented to someone else.

✔ Many institutions generate lists or databases to help students find off-campus housing. This is a good place to begin, but it offers no assurance of fair treatment.

✔ A majority of institutions *do not* offer advice to students or their parents about lease terms or other contractual obligations, so you must seek such advice on your own.

✔ Some student government groups compile housing lists with student reactions to particular situations and advice to potential renters.

✔ Sometimes minority students new to a majority campus are less connected and have fewer resources than their white peers, so they tend to take less desirable housing. The facts are that most minority student renters treat their apartments or rooms more respectfully than white students. In spite of the research, numerous white landlords still refuse to believe this.

✔ Do not automatically drop all defense mechanisms when coming into a college town for the first time. Even though they might be few in number, there may be unscrupulous individuals ready to prey on unsuspecting and trusting first-semester students.

✔ The chief difference between renting in cities as opposed to rural settings is that there are probably fewer cons being run in rural areas, but there is also less support for the renter, such as the government rent-control agencies that operate in large urban areas.

✔ Most students do not know their rights or obligations in renting, or even with on-campus housing contracts.

✔ *Document, document, document.* Record all names, dates, witnesses, the gist of conversations, verbal agreements, and the like. Get everything you can in writing.

✔ Know what you are signing: Read it carefully. For example, know which utilities are paid by the landlord and which by the renter, and whether there is a grace period for rent payment.

✔ In the final analysis, it is probably more expensive to live off campus than in institutional housing, but there are perceived benefits of independent living that make it very attractive to a large numbers of students.

The bottom line is always this: *Caveat emptor—buyer beware!* Leases are designed to protect the apartment owner, not the renter.

**Living at Home**    The third alternative for students is to choose a school near their parents and continue living at home. This option presents a number of problems while solving others. Let's examine the positive side first.

Living at home provides continuity and familiarity. If your relationship with your son or daughter is mutually satisfying, their living at home and going to school can be a workable arrangement. Both you and your child will need to consider a number of changes, however.

For the student, schoolwork takes on added importance. There are new demands on her time and attention, and seemingly less time for family matters. It may appear as though you have a boarder, not a child.

Here are a few things to keep in mind if you are thinking of having your child live at home while attending college:

- ✔ By having your student live at home, you may be able to save up to 30 percent of the total cost of his education.

- ✔ Your student may not reap the benefits of a full college experience. (Some parents actually see this as a plus.)

- ✔ Many times eighteen and nineteen year olds will test the limits of their newfound independence, which could lead to tension at home.

- ✔ Make sure there is a clearly defined set of rules. It is still your home! This is especially important when setting ground rules about guests.

- ✔ You can consider some arrangement for room and board expenses if your student is receiving financial aid in excess of the cost of tuition and books. Even if the money exchange is nominal, it does establish a pattern of fiscal responsibility.

- ✔ Many parents find that they cannot expect too much in the way of help around the house, especially if their student is paying for room and board. Younger siblings might grow to resent this seeming inequity.

- ✔ Be aware that during exam periods, students are especially anxious and prone to fly off at the least provocation.

- ✔ Even if your eighteen year old is living at home and you claim her as a tax exemption, you do not have any more legal rights to information about her life. You may wish to negotiate some arrangement, however, as a condition for her living at home, such as having access to her grades.

- ✔ You have the right to limit or prohibit alcohol or drugs in your home.

- ✔ Consider some form of periodic review of the arrangement.

# Parents' Legal Rights

This is the issue that is most vexing to parents. On the one hand, a high percentage of parents are paying some or all of the costs of educating their children; and on the other hand, they find that their legal rights regarding their children are quite suddenly very restricted. What happened? It's really very simple: Your matriculating sons and daughters have recently turned eighteen years old; in the eyes of the law, they are no longer dependent minors, but emancipated adults.

But, you may argue, he still lives at home, eats my food, uses my car, and gets an allowance. Nevertheless, the reality is that other than for income tax purposes, where you may still be able to claim him as an exemption, he is free of your legal guardianship.

What does your new status mean to you as a parent? Here are a few of the major relationship differences:

- ✔ In general, you no longer have absolute legal access to any school records without the written approval of your son or daughter. This includes, but is not limited to, grades, progress reports, failing notices, official enrollment status at the institution (including notices of expulsion or academic dismissal), medical records or treatment information, disciplinary records, and even address and phone number if the student requests that such information not be made public.

- ✔ School officials can be held legally liable for unauthorized release of student information, except in cases where there is evidence of some immediate and serious threat to the physical or psychological well-being of the student. Sometimes school officials must make a judgment call in these matters, but routinely they will come down on the side of student confidentiality.

- ✔ You may arrange to see many school records, counselors, or advisers by having your child sign a release document that spells out exactly to what information or persons your student is willing to grant you access.

- ✔ Be aware that the rules and laws binding different professionals to confidentiality vary by both profession and state.

- ✔ School officials may contact you without prior permission if there is imminent danger of your child causing injury to others.

✔ In some special programs, students will be required to sign a general release of information as part of the acceptance process, which gives program staff access to parents and vice versa. Even with these releases, counselors and advisers are usually quite conservative with regard to the kind of student information they release.

✔ Any legal contract entered into by your eighteen-year-old son or daughter that you have not signed for as a guarantor or co-signer is solely their responsibility. This includes installment credit, such as Visa, MasterCard, and department-store charge cards; auto or commercial bank loans; or other types of personal loans. This also applies to leases.

For further information on this subject, you can consult The Family Educational Rights and Privacy Act of 1974, available on the Internet or from your local library. This document spells out many of the rights of eighteen-year-old students enrolled in post-secondary institutions.

# Parents' Role After Matriculation

Once your son or daughter is safely installed in a residence-hall room or apartment, your role as a parent changes but does not become any less important. To fulfill your mission as chief cheerleader and sometimes adviser, there are several matters of which you should be aware, in particular the problems of drugs and alcohol on campuses.

## Campus Police, Drugs, and Alcohol

Although we may not enjoy considering the issues of drugs and alcohol, they are unfortunate realities on college campuses. This section aims to clarify these issues for parents and describes how college campuses address them.

✔ Campus police have a dual function: They serve as a conventional police force and also provide public safety services and education.

✔ Thankfully, most on-campus police forces do not combat a steady stream of violent crime. Instead they engage in a good deal of crime prevention and risk reduction education.

✔ Both majority and minority views of campus police are generally negative, but for different reasons. Attitude surveys consistently demonstrate that white students have negative opinions about campus police just because they are cops, whereas African American and Latino students hold the same negative opinions but because they view campus police as racist.

✔ More than 85 percent of cases brought to campus police involve alcohol.

✔ A student stands only a 1-in-20 chance of running afoul of the campus police while in college. This figure includes traffic offenses, which constitute the vast majority of student infractions.

✔ Drug use on college campuses is up. This is especially true of marijuana, which has become more socially acceptable among young adults. Don't assume that just because a school is rural drugs won't be readily available.

✔ According to a number of university security officials, the penalty for marijuana use on campus is not generally as severe as in the outside community. For example, simple use might result in a warning for a first or even second offense and be handled completely internally. Penalties for selling are much more serious.

✔ Although colleges and universities have somewhat more informal judicial systems than society at large, a college student who breaks the law can be subject to a form of double jeopardy; he or she may have to face university sanctions as well as penalties of the civil or criminal justice systems.

✔ As in society in general, computer crimes are rising dramatically on campuses across the nation. For some reason, the unauthorized or illegal use of computers is not thought of as criminal by large segments of the population.

✔ Cases of racial and ethnic intolerance are treated more severely on college campuses than in society in general. They may even be cause for dismissal from an institution. Nevertheless, hate crimes are up significantly on college campuses, again mirroring society at large.

✔ There is not much you can do to prevent alcohol or drug use if your son or daughter is determined to indulge. More than 50 percent of all college-age individuals admit to some experimentation with marijuana, and the percentage who try alcohol is even higher. Your only preventive measure is to talk openly about the subject before your child actually begins classes.

✔ As a rule, college campuses are safer than the outside communities, even in urban areas.

## Staying Involved

Even when your children are college students, your involvement is vital to their success. Though they may seem to want you to keep out of their lives, don't. Admittedly, there is a fine line to be drawn here, and it is sometimes difficult for a parent to know just when to butt out and when to intervene. To some extent it depends upon the relationship you and your child have and your confidence in his or her ability to make sound, mature judgments. Let's discuss two specific situations that bear on the subject at hand.

*Once your child has gone away to school, when do you take the initiative to call if he hasn't called you first?* There is no pat answer to this question. Suffice it to say that if you haven't heard from him in a few weeks, it's time to check in. To help their kids stay in touch, some parents give a supply of prestamped, preaddressed post cards to send home. Others provide a long-distance calling card (with potentially dangerous results, if my children are any example). Whatever you intend to do, let your student know in advance so he doesn't think you are invading his privacy.

*Should you visit your child on campus?* Of course you should! But, again, a visit should take place with plenty of advance notice. A useful strategy is to let your student suggest a time and agenda. Nothing can be quite so disastrous as an unscheduled family visit soon after a student's arrival on campus. Since most schools schedule parents' days, this could prove to be an excellent opportunity for a visit.

There are other particularly stressful times when you should make a point to contact your child. February in the snow belt, for instance, can be especially depressing just because of the weather. Midterm exams come along at about the fourth- and eighth-week point in a fourteen- or fifteen-week semester. Also, the week immediately after the last day of class is a high-anxiety time for most students, with final exams either being prepared for or taking place. You don't have to make a big production out of letting your children know that you are pulling for them. A "care package" of favorite cookies or cake with an encouraging note is enough. If you don't know when these times and other potentially high-anxiety periods are, just call the school and ask to speak to any counselor. These professionals will know the approximate dates.

Sooner or later your child will decide to pay a visit to the old homestead. After only a few hours you may be tempted to remark on how he has changed. You may recognize a cynicism about traditional values you hold near and dear. Your child now questions everything. He doesn't want to spend time with you, but rather is out of the house almost immediately, looking for friends. You barely see him at all. Come Sunday he vigorously declines the opportunity for you to show him off in church. I'm sure you get the picture. You may remember that you went through a period in your youth that must have appeared just about the same to your parents. Have heart, friends, there is hope yet.

Almost every student goes through a period where old values and beliefs are no longer sufficient or valid. The surprise is that many return to them eventually, some sooner than others. This is not true for everyone, however; for some of the ideas students are exposed to early on in their college careers do make a profound and positive impression on them. These ideas can completely change how they view the world. Any type of post-secondary education can and often is a time of dramatic change. You need to prepare yourself for it.

# Personal Observations: From One Parent to Another

This chapter closes with the following collection of comments, advice, and experiences of advisers, faculty, and parents of several minority students who have recently completed one or more years of post-secondary education. Bear in mind that these comments are in no particular order of importance and should be considered selectively by you as parents of a minority student.

✔ Parents who themselves have had experience with education after high school tend to be more involved in their child's educational decisions.

✔ Many parents of students in large urban areas have told me that they have difficulty looking at the big picture; that is, they don't see the eventual benefits of education. For them, just getting their kid out of the neighborhood is enough.

✔ Some parents may not realize what it takes to succeed in college: It's a job that involves between 40 and 50 hours of work inside and outside the classroom to just make B's. In high school most work was concentrated within the classroom. Just the opposite is true in college, and in many other types of post-secondary schools for that matter. Students spend an average of only fifteen to eighteen hours in class but are required to study at least twice that length of time outside of class.

✔ The competition in class can be fierce and is often disabling.

✔ You should encourage your child to consider all the academic opportunities presented to him or her. Things like study abroad, a semester at sea, internships in business and industry, co-op programs, research with professors, work study programs, and so on can be excellent opportunities and are widely available, especially at large schools.

✔ Affirmative action status will determine in large measure the climate for minorities on predominantly white campuses.

✔ Parents may need to consider that even though their child did well in high school, she could find herself noncompetitive in some college programs.

✔ From my twenty-five years of experience, I have found that numbers of minority students end up attending predominantly white institutions because their families have adopted mainstream values and lifestyles.

✔ Some students could face the prospect of having to balance their fit into the old neighborhood or town and their response to the new values of a college experience.

✔ In addition to the transition all other students need to make, a main issue for minority students at majority institutions is contending with negative discrimination.

✔ Some white students and staff see minorities as threats.

✔ A minority student's coping skills will determine how much of a toll racism will take on academic performance.

✔ Multiracial students face specific and unique problems, such as no defined support system, clubs, or fraternities specific to multiracial students. Parents of these students therefore need to help them come to some understanding of who they are and where they belong.

✔ Many minority groups see so-called self-segregation as self-protection.

✔ Many Asian students prefer to be identified by their national origin.

✔ Minority-specific Greek organizations (fraternities and sororities) can be positive if they do not totally restrict a student's interaction with others.

✔ There is a stereotype that Asian parents are overdemanding, and the notion that Asian students are discouraged for going into the arts is not borne out by the evidence.

✔ Parents should attempt to forge a relationship with a faculty or staff member at their student's school and encourage their son or daughter to do the same. In her now classic book, *Blacks in College*, author Jackie Fleming proposed that those minority students who forged a strong, personal relationship with a faculty member or key administrator showed far greater persistence. In other words, they had a much better than average chance of success. As a matter of priority, you should encourage your child to seek such individuals out!

Finally, I urge you to examine other chapters of this book and discuss them with your son or daughter. Such talks can prove extremely enlightening to both of you. Often you'll be surprised at the problems that concern your prospective student; but with your caring involvement, you can help your son or daughter choose the right college and thrive there.

# Reference

Fleming, Jackie. *Blacks in College: A Comparative Study of Students' Success in Black and White Institutions* (San Francisco: Jossey-Bass, 1984).

# Chapter 3

# How to Put Skills into Your Studying

**Michael Blanco and Marc Levey**

*"Study Skills." It even sounds boring. Since studying itself is boring, "studying" about studying must be even worse. Who's got the time?*

**N**o doubt about it, study skills have a bad reputation today. And why not? What other topic can turn your brain into putty in five minutes? For most students, getting study skills is like getting a disease. Only nerds need study skills.

But when you think about it, it makes sense to look at study strategies. Who would attempt to become a professional athlete or musician without studying the professional's techniques? Maybe a few top-notch athletes or musicians make it without working hard on every aspect of their "game," but for most, greatness comes only when attention is given to all the details of the performance. The same holds true for success in college. Maybe a few of your friends get straight A's without much effort, but for the rest of us, we need to look carefully at our study skills to make sure we're getting the most from our efforts. This chapter will help you practice tried-and-true techniques to improve your study skills.

## The ABC's of Study Skills

You can use lots of different study skills to achieve your academic goals. Some of these are just plain common sense, yet many students ignore them. Common sense study skills include going to every class, sitting up front, asking questions and interacting with classmates, not waiting until the last minute to do your work, turning in assignments on time, doing your work neatly and completely, and many others. You may not want to do some of these things, however, because you feel threatened by the class or campus environment and you don't want to stand out any more than you have to. The fact is, though, that not doing some of these things may make you stand out in the wrong way to the wrong person, namely, your professor. Especially when you are a minority student at a predominantly white campus, when you're not in class it's probably noticed more than when others are absent, and if you never ask a question in class, for instance, it's going to be more obvious to the professor. You may make yourself more noticed by your absence and lack of involvement than by being present, up front, and involved.

Below is a list of behaviors and techniques that will improve almost everyone's performance in college. Put a ✓ next to the ones that you use now, put an ✗ next to the ones you think might work for you, and leave blank those that you think would be a waste of time. Carefully consider your choices and your reasons for making them; it will tell you a lot about your study skills and your capacity for improving them.

_____ I go to every class on time every day.

_____ I sit up front in class.

_____ I turn in all assignments on time.

_____ I have learned to use a word processor.

_____ I type or use a word processor for all assignments when possible.

_____ I make sure every assignment I do represents my best effort.

_____ I do all assigned readings *before* the class period they are due.

_____ I see my academic adviser at least once per semester.

_____ I find a new academic adviser if I don't connect well with my current one.

_____ I find a person (counselor, professor) to mentor me who is not my academic adviser.

_____ I visit with each one of my professors at least once per semester to discuss some aspect of the course.

_____ I set up a daily schedule and follow it carefully.

_____ I buy a daily planner and write down all my appointments.

_____ I study at least two hours outside of class for every hour I spend in class.

_____ I finish all long-term assignments (i.e., term papers) at least a day or two before they are due.

_____ I get as much studying done as possible *before* 8:00 P.M.

_____ I get as much studying done as possible before the weekend.

_____ I begin to study for tests at least one week in advance.

_____ I complete at least 50 percent of my studying for all tests before my final study day prior to the test.

_____ I find a spot away from distractions that I use for studying only.

_____ I spend a few minutes *reviewing* my class notes as soon as possible after class.

_____ I spend a few minutes *previewing* class notes before each class.

_____ I don't study for more than two hours without taking a break.

_____ I find out what resources my campus has for helping students (particularly students of color) and visit them at least once.

_____ I make friends with people who get good grades.

_____ I form study groups for my toughest classes.

_____ I take organized notes.

_____ I take a freshman seminar if my college offers one.

_____ I get a job (on campus if possible) where I work no more than 15 hours per week.

_____ I get involved in at least one campus or community organization.

# Time Management: When and How Much

College will demand that you develop a personal game plan for organizing your time, notes, activities, and priorities. In high school your life was largely planned by your school schedule, family, and the habits you had developed since childhood. College is very different. You probably live in a different place and have a different "family" (your roommate and close friends). You class schedule doesn't take up your entire day every day, and you are probably more independent from your parents and family than before. The only way to cope with all these changes and new demands is to learn to control your environment rather than let your environment control you.

One of the most critical aspects of college is *time management*—the "when and how much" of your new environment. Different people have different ideas about time management, and these differences can work against you. For example, you may not think it's a big deal to walk into class five minutes late, but your professor may take it as a personal insult. You probably already know you'll need to study more in college than in high school, but because you also have many more options for how to use your time, vital study time can often get squeezed out. In college you will need to think about time management more precisely than you have in the past.

Time management may be the most important skill you'll need for success in college. Students who manage their time well accomplish more in less time and have more time for doing things they like. Many good time management programs exist, and every program is based upon a very simple idea: Make a daily schedule and *stick to it.* Simply making a schedule and following it is not enough, however. *How* you plan your time is also important. Many students run into time management problems because they don't get enough done soon enough. Although some students claim that they work best under pressure, often they don't realize how well they actually could do if they had the time to do a thorough job on all their work.

## How High School Makes It Difficult for You to Manage Your Time in College

If you have a problem with time management, you're not alone. You've been "programmed" by your high school studies to manage your time poorly. As incredible as this sounds, in a sense high school (in fact, grades K–12) prepares you to fail in college, in terms of time management. It doesn't matter if you are from a "good" or "bad" school district, or if you got an A in calculus or did your best in PE. The problem is not the subjects you learned; it's how you were taught to manage your learning time for twelve years. The college learning process is very different from anything you encountered in high school.

Compare the charts on the next two pages to see how different the college learning experience is and how differently your day is structured. A typical day in college differs from high school in at least two ways: (1) you are in class about half the time, and (2) your class times are usually spread out, with gaps between classes that can be several hours long. Also note that the total academic time (i.e., time devoted to class, homework, and studying) is not that different between high school and college, even though the latter includes far less time in class. Assuming that high school students are in class 5 to 6 hours per day and do 1 to 2 hours of homework per evening, students in high school spend 35 to 40 hours of academic time per week. For college students who have 15 to 16 credit hours (1 credit

# Differences Between the High School and the College Learning Processes

| The High School<br>Learning Process | The College<br>Learning Process |
|---|---|
| Classes—<br>five days a week, five to six hours per day (25–30 hours total) | Classes—<br>random, 15–16 credits per week on average (12.5–13.5 hours total) |
| Teachers—<br>professional educators whose primary job is to help you learn | Teachers—<br>not necessarily trained as educators; primary job is often research |
| Pace of classes—<br>deliberate and methodical; designed to teach you most of the material in class | Pace of classes—<br>very fast, designed to cover large amounts of material in as short a time as possible |
| Homework—<br>reinforces what is learned in the classroom | Homework—<br>intended as a primary mode of learning |

hour equals 50 minutes in class) and study 2 hours for every hour in class (about 25 to 27 hours per week), their total academic time will be somewhere between 37 and 41 hours per week.

## How to Spend Your Time Effectively

So, in terms of time management, what's the difference between high school and college? It's *how* you spend your time. In high school you do very little work outside of class. Homework is used not so much for learning as for reinforcing what you've already learned. In college your professors will expect you to do much of the learning on your own through problem solving, reading, research, writing, projects, labs, and other academic activities. That's partly why you spend less time in class even though you learn more. Of course, college learning

# How These Differences
# Affect Your Use of Time

| Typical High School Day | Typical College Day |
|---|---|
| 7:00 A.M.—Get up | 7:00 A.M.—Get up |
| 8:30 A.M.–3:00 P.M.—School | 8:00–8:50 A.M.—Class |
| 3:00–5:00 P.M.—Activities/work | 8:50–11:15 A.M.—"Free" time |
| 5:00–6:00 P.M.—Dinner | 11:15 A.M.–12:05 P.M.—Class |
| 6:00–8:00 P.M.—Homework/study | 12:30 P.M.–2:30 P.M.—"Free" time |
| 8:00–11:00 P.M.—Evening activities | 2:30–3:20 P.M.—Class |
| | 3:30 P.M.—"Free" time |
| Total weekly academic time: 30–40 hours per week (25–30 hours of class time per week plus 5–10 hours of homework time) | Total Weekly Academic Time: 37.5–40.5 hours (15–16 credits) per week (12.5–13.5 hours of class time per week plus 2 hours of homework for every hour in class, i.e., 25–27 hours) |

also involves a faster pace and more sophisticated material. The work you do on your own makes up for the fewer hours in class.

Make sense so far? Well, here's the rub: Where are you going to put all those extra hours you need to spend studying on your own? In high school, other than in study hall, students do all their homework after they finish school for the day. Often high school students don't begin doing homework until the evening, perhaps late in the evening. Some successful high school students claim they never do homework at all. Unfortunately, many students follow this pattern in college without realizing that the rules of the game have changed completely. Remember, you need to study, on average, twenty-five to twenty-seven hours per week outside of class, or five to six hours each day. If you begin your study time in the evening, you can see that it could take you until after midnight every evening to complete your work (not a good idea, especially if you have physics at 8:00 the next morning).

Fortunately, there's a solution. To get all your work done without being dead on your feet the next day, you've got to study during the "free" time between your classes during the day. Many college students waste this time watching TV, playing video games, etc. You don't have to study every moment between classes to use your time effectively, but the more time you devote to your books during the day, the less you'll have to do in the evening. With proper planning and an early start on studying, you can have all your work done early enough in the evening to still have some time for yourself.

One caution, though: Planning and starting early assumes that you're willing to devote enough time to studying and that you have the commitment and discipline to spend twenty-five to thirty-five hours per week studying outside of class. Research indicates that many students expect to get at least a B average on ten hours of studying per week or less. As you might guess, very few of these students attain their goals. The bottom line in time management is: *You must be willing to devote at least two hours of study outside of class for every hour in class.*

Another way some college students mismanage time is by not using their study time efficiently. Many students put off their work so long that the only way they can get it done on time is by pulling off "all nighters" or other marathon study sessions. Some students believe this method works best because they get their studying done all at once and don't have to waste time by "going over stuff" again and again. Although this approach may seem best on the surface, in fact, the opposite is true. As the chart on the next page demonstrates, instead of getting things done all at once, the efficiency of the mind decreases the longer you work without taking a break.

Notice that immediately after you begin to study, your efficiency begins to drop. After two hours of solid study, most people are accomplishing far less than they were able to initially. They have dropped so far down on the "learning curve" that they'd be better off taking a break and, say, getting some exercise. Even a fifteen-minute walk around the dorm will help get your mind and body refreshed so that you can be more effective in your use of study time. If it's late at night, the negative effect of long hours of study increases. If you have a test the next day, you've been studying for six hours straight, and it's 2:00

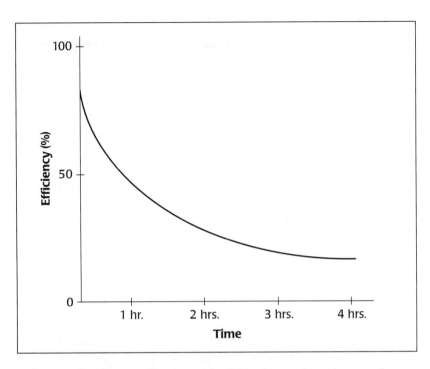

A.M., you'd be better off going to bed. You're not learning much anyway, and sleep will probably help you prepare for the test more than studying at this point.

## A Rule of Thumb: Shorter Is Better

Considering the learning-curve dilemma detailed in the previous section, the best way to learn is to take breaks between study sessions to give your mind a rest. For most tasks it's best to take a short break (5 to 10 minutes) every 45 to 60 minutes, and then take a longer break (at least a half hour) after two or three hours of studying. During longer breaks it's great to do something physical: Go jogging or take a walk, play some basketball or volleyball, or do whatever else you like. This will not only give your brain a break, it will refresh you physically so that you can return to studying with a better sense of well-being. Of course, these longer breaks need to be moderate. Besides the fact that you need to get back to your desk in time to get as much done as possible, most people can't play basketball for four hours and come back refreshed. Another way to use time effectively is to plan an activity for these longer breaks. After you've put in some study time, go to a club meeting or dinner, and then come back for another session. This means that you'll need a lot of self-discipline to say no to the dozens of distractions that can get you off track.

Okay, let's say you buy this idea for long-term projects or major tests that must be worked on over several days. But what about things that don't take so much time? Let's say, for example, you have a test tomorrow, but all the material can be easily covered in several hours, and you have plenty of time the day before the test. You can cover the material before it gets too late, and you even have enough time to take some breaks. Then it would be best to do all your studying the day before the test, right?

Wrong. Research indicates that you remember best when you study in small chunks several days before the test. In other words, if you had only five hours to study for a test and no more, you would be better off studying an hour a day for five days than studying for five hours the day before the test. The brain remembers best when it has some time to pull together information and relate it to something you have learned beforehand. It's something like training for long-distance running. If you knew you were going to run a ten-kilometer race a month from now, you might decide to train for the race by running two miles a day for thirty days prior to the race, which would amount to sixty miles for your training. But, let's say you put off your training until the day before the race. To run sixty miles the day before the race would obviously *not* help you; in fact, you'd probably end up in the hospital! Yet some students somehow think they can do all their studying at once in preparing for tests. They put in marathon study sessions for most of the night and then wonder why they don't do well.

The "shorter the better" rule of thumb doesn't work just for tests, either. Reading comprehension is also improved by reading in short bursts. One of the worst ways to read a chapter in a textbook is to simply start on the first page and then read the chapter straight on through. You're much better off to map out the chapter first and then read it in segments that are shorter and easier to understand. We examine this more later in this chapter.

# Using a Daily Planner to Help You Manage Time Effectively

One of the best ways to manage your time is with a daily planner. As a time management tool, try this exercise: Using the daily planner on the following page, put together a schedule for yourself for one week. Use what you have learned so far to put together a schedule that will use your time most effectively. Be sure to schedule all of the following:

1. Enough time for studying (two hours outside of class for every hour in class)

2. At least half of your "free" time between classes for studying

3. No more than two hours of studying without a break of at least thirty minutes

4. No more than four hours of studying on the weekend (you can, of course, study more on the weekend, but to be safe and realistic don't plan to study more than four hours)

# College Classes and Homework

How much you study and when you do it are vital to college success. But it's just as important to study the right things in the right way. In other words, the "what and how" are just as important as the "when and how much." Again, high school does not prepare you well for dealing with the new realities of studying in college. Most college classes are structured very differently from high school classes.

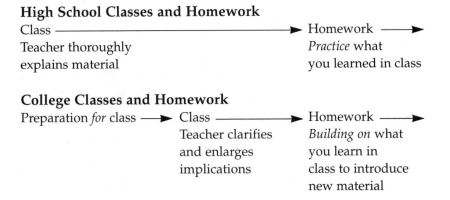

### High School Classes and Homework
Class ⟶ Homework ⟶
Teacher thoroughly          *Practice* what
explains material           you learned in class

### College Classes and Homework
Preparation *for* class ⟶ Class ⟶ Homework ⟶
                          Teacher clarifies      *Building on* what
                          and enlarges           you learn in
                          implications           class to introduce
                                                 new material

# Daily Planner

| | SUN | MON | TUES | WED | THURS | FRI | SAT |
|---|---|---|---|---|---|---|---|
| 6:00 A.M. | | | | | | | |
| 6:30 A.M. | | | | | | | |
| 7:00 A.M. | | | | | | | |
| 7:30 A.M. | | | | | | | |
| 8:00 A.M. | | | | | | | |
| 8:30 A.M. | | | | | | | |
| 9:00 A.M. | | | | | | | |
| 9:30 A.M. | | | | | | | |
| 10:00 A.M. | | | | | | | |
| 10:30 A.M. | | | | | | | |
| 11:00 A.M. | | | | | | | |
| 11:30 A.M. | | | | | | | |
| 12:00 P.M. | | | | | | | |
| 12:30 P.M. | | | | | | | |
| 1:00 P.M. | | | | | | | |
| 1:30 P.M. | | | | | | | |
| 2:00 P.M. | | | | | | | |
| 2:30 P.M. | | | | | | | |
| 3:00 P.M. | | | | | | | |
| 3:30 P.M. | | | | | | | |
| 4:00 P.M. | | | | | | | |
| 4:30 P.M. | | | | | | | |
| 5:00 P.M. | | | | | | | |
| 5:30 P.M. | | | | | | | |
| 6:00 P.M. | | | | | | | |
| 6:30 P.M. | | | | | | | |
| 7:00 P.M. | | | | | | | |
| 7:30 P.M. | | | | | | | |
| 8:00 P.M. | | | | | | | |
| 8:30 P.M. | | | | | | | |
| 9:00 P.M. | | | | | | | |
| 9:30 P.M. | | | | | | | |
| 10:00 P.M. | | | | | | | |
| 10:30 P.M. | | | | | | | |
| 11:00 P.M. | | | | | | | |
| 11:30 P.M. | | | | | | | |

**High School**  In high school you are not necessarily expected to know anything about the class discussion beforehand beyond what you've already learned previously in class and practiced through homework.

**College**  In college you are often expected to do some reading or other preparation on the material to be presented in class.

**High School**  In high school the teacher will guide you through almost everything you need to learn during class. If you don't know anything about the material for class beforehand, this will not usually affect your learning in the class.

**College**  In college the teacher will often present the lesson in a way that assumes you already have some basic understanding of the material based on your prior preparation. If you don't have the understanding, you may not be able to comprehend what the instructor presents in class, which will put you even farther behind.

**High School**  In high school homework is mainly used to practice what you've learned in class. The assignment may be more difficult, but it will not typically go beyond what you learned in class.

**College**  In college homework is used to build on what you've learned in class. The problems not only may be more difficult than what you learned in class, but they may go beyond the material presented in class.

To appreciate the significance of these differences, consider the following scenario: A student takes a college course where preparation is expected for the class, and homework will build on the class discussion to introduce new material. Unfortunately, the student uses study methods learned in high school. This student typically does not prepare well for class and may not do any homework. If she or he does any of the assignment, the goal may be to "just get by."

The student now arrives in class unprepared for the lecture. Because the professor is basing her presentation on material that she assumes students have covered before class, she does not define key terms and concepts as precisely as she would were she presenting them for the first time.

For most students in this situation, it's already too late. Most of us would be hopelessly lost. In the world of the college classroom, if a student doesn't understand exactly the basic idea behind a concept (which is often contained in some key word or phrase), he will probably not understand anything about how that concept is used. If the professor then proceeds to discuss more ideas based on other concepts that are all tied into the original concept that should have been learned before class, and our student never bothered to study that concept before the lecture ... well, you can see how the student would soon be completely left behind. Instead of class being a rewarding learning experience, it becomes a major frustration. From this experience a major enemy of success—self-doubt—begins to creep into the student's mind.

Now let's say our student knows he is in trouble and decides to do the homework to "catch up." Because homework is based on what is learned in class, the assignment may be very difficult to do now. If the assignment includes questions or problems that ask the student to apply major concepts of the lecture in new and different ways, he will probably have even more trouble and may not complete the questions or problems with a thorough understanding of what he has done. Because the homework assignment is not done well again, the student falls behind even more. The vicious cycle begins to repeat itself until finally the student decides to not go to class anymore. Viewed a certain way, this decision makes sense, because the student no longer sees class as a helpful experience. But because the course is a requirement, he attempts to get lecture notes from a friend and take the test. Disaster follows, and the student is forced to either drop the class or try to limp along, only to get a D or, even worse, an F.

Although this story is fiction, it has happened in some form to thousands of students who simply did not change their behavior because they failed to recognize the fundamental differences between high school and college learning. Obviously, students who prepare for class thoroughly and complete their assignments with a full understanding of the material will do much better in their classes, even in courses that are not structured exactly as described here. These successful students understand what they need to do to master the classroom and take charge of their new environment.

### "But I Knew the Material!"

Listen to student reactions as college test scores are posted, and what you often hear is something like, "But I knew the material!" Students often don't understand *how well* professors expect them to know the material or how professors may expect them to *apply* the material.

College professors expect you to so thoroughly understand the subject matter that they ask questions that are not only very complex and detailed, but that also will find out how well you can use what you know.

The following question from a college examination demonstrates these points.

*Consider the following system:*

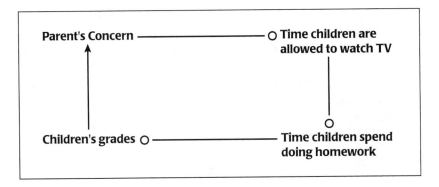

*The relationship between the parents' concern and the time children are allowed to watch television is an example of:*

a.  *an equilibrium point*

b.  *a positive coupling*

c.  *a perturbation*

d.  *a negative coupling*

You may have thought that this question was for a psychology or sociology course but, in fact, it is from a science test! The professor is asking students to understand very complex concepts and apply them to situations that have nothing directly to do with science. This simple example demonstrates that in high school, knowledge and skills are enough; but in college, mastery, comprehension, and abstract reasoning ability are necessary.

# Hyperlearning

One of the most important ideas for college success is *hyperlearning*. Hyperlearning will help you gain the mastery that college professors are looking for when they write exams, and it will help you connect what you learn to other ideas. In other words, hyperlearning helps you go beyond the typical "but I knew the material" attitude to *really* knowing the material.

In essence, hyperlearning involves not stopping once you have simply learned something. Most often students are satisfied once they memorize a list, do a problem, complete an assignment, or read a chapter. These activities may be necessary, of course, but they are really only the beginning of learning, and you should expect no more than a C if you stop there. Continuing the learning process involves two steps. First you need to *review the material on a regular basis* so that your mind has a chance to comprehend fully what you're trying to learn. Next you need to take some time to think through what you have reviewed until you *internalize the material.* In other words, you need to own it. At this point, the subject almost becomes part of you, and you may feel like you would want to teach it to someone else if you could.

### Review and Save Time

By now you're probably thinking: I don't have the time for all this! I'm having a hard enough time just staying on top of things I have to do! One of the amazing benefits of periodically reviewing material is that it doesn't require a lot of time to be effective. In fact, when done properly you can actually save time by regularly reviewing your class notes and readings. In order to understand this, you need to understand how your mind forgets and remembers.

The first chart on the next page demonstrates what happens to information you learn over time.

Notice that after a month (just about the typical time between tests in college), you've forgotten about 80 percent of what you initially learned. No wonder studying for tests in college can take so long and produce such poor results! You can study all night for a test and still only scratch the surface of what you need to know. But look at the next chart to see what happens if material is reviewed just once a week.

These charts show that your brain is a powerful learning engine if you give it a chance. When properly fed, the brain has amazing capabilities for recall, learning, and analysis. But what do many students do? Starve it for a month, and then try to stuff it full in one evening. Your brain isn't designed to work this way, and the result is typically a bad grade and a lot of frustration.

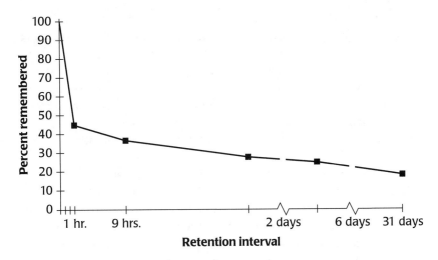

Memory: No Review

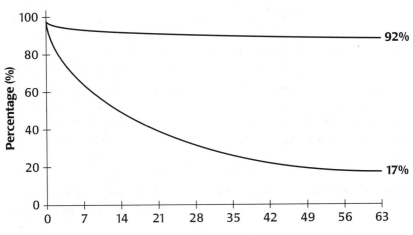

Memory: Weekly Review

Fortunately, the solution is fairly simple: If you review your class notes, readings, and assignments once a week *for a very short time,* you'll be amazed at how much you already know when the test rolls around. This review can be done during the four hours of study you planned for the weekend, and it doesn't even need to take four hours.

Scan your class notes, look over previous homework assignments, and work out a few problems again. Read the portions of your textbook that you have highlighted or made notes on and ask your roommate to drill you. When you sit down to study for the test, you'll find that you won't need to spend time orienting yourself to material you haven't covered in weeks, and you can get right down to studying the material for full comprehension. Using this process, a weekly review can be completed in less than two hours and can have a dramatic effect on your test results.

Some students find that they get increased benefits by recopying and organizing their notes. This practice has the effect of acting as a review while you put your notes into a more understandable format. Then, when you go to study for the test, your notes are fresher in your mind and easier to follow. Logically, students learn better and faster from notes that are well organized and easily read.

### Take a Minute to Review/Preview

Another powerful hyperlearning memory device is the "review/preview" cycle, which is done on a daily basis with readings and class notes. After each class take five minutes to review the notes you just took. The next day arrive at class ten minutes early, take out your notes, and read over the previous lecture again. Take no more than five minutes. Then review your reading assignment from the night before; again, take five minutes to scan headings, portions you highlighted, chapter summaries, and notes you made to yourself in the text. This exercise, which takes no more than ten minutes, has the effect of "priming" your brain for the lecture. You are now ready to learn and are completely oriented to the subject at hand. This practice will plant a few "hooks" in your brain so that when you go to do the assignment or read the text, you'll be able to learn the material more easily, simply because you reviewed the topic briefly.

## Taking Good Notes: Are Those Your Class Notes or Chicken Scratch?

This chapter has already mentioned the importance of class notes, and with good reason. Your class notes are your lifeline to the class, and most of what you will be responsible for learning in class will come from your notes. Therefore, how you approach them is vital to your success. Problems with class notes generally fall into three categories: sloppiness, poor organization, and too much detail.

Handwriting is the culprit of the first problem, but most students don't understand how poor handwriting affects them. They reason: Hey, I can read my writing even if nobody else can, so what's the big deal? The big deal is that even though you can probably read it right after the lecture, you may have difficulty weeks later when you go to study for an exam. And even if you can read it, you may be wasting valuable time deciphering your handwriting when you should be learning the material. Of course, poor handwriting is the result of years of poor writing habits and isn't solved overnight. But most students can write more neatly if they try, especially if they practice improving their handwriting outside of class. Ultimately, the best solution may be to rewrite or type your notes as soon as possible after class. This has several benefits: In addition to reviewing the material, you are also improving your notes because you are able to think about the content in a more relaxed setting and organize your notes accordingly.

Poor organization is sloppiness in relating one point in your notes to the other points. Ideas don't exist by themselves—they relate to other ideas—and your notes should reflect these relationships. Many students use traditional outline form to show how ideas relate, but other methods exist that are just as effective. Avoid taking notes that simply list one point after another as if each idea stands by itself. Studying from notes that show no relationships among ideas may give you the facts of the lecture, but you won't know how those facts fit within the overall context. So when your instructor asks questions on the test that examine these relationships, you'll be in trouble.

Many students are frantic about the possibility of missing a point in the lecture: When they take notes, they become recording secretaries instead of active learners. The root issue for this problem is listening. True listening is hard work; you have to concentrate on what is being said and make decisions about what it means and how important it is. Because it's easier to just write down everything, students end up cheating themselves of true learning: They're taking dictation instead of listening and processing the information. If they don't get the gist of the lecture in class, it certainly won't be any clearer later on from reading the notes. The result is little learning but lots of notes. Students make the mistake of being less concerned about what the notes mean, priding themselves instead on their sheer volume. The result of this copious note-taking is reams of paper that they don't understand.

Doesn't it make more sense to concentrate on what's being said in the lecture, make decisions about what it means and what's most important, and write down those ideas and examples that are central to the professor's presentation? This method has the additional benefit of giving you more time to write neater and better organize your thoughts on paper.

Fortunately, there's a simple but effective technique that allows you to deal with all three of these problems at once. It's called the Cornell format of note-taking.

## Note-Taking Using the Cornell Format

Instead of using the whole page when you take class notes, draw a vertical line at about the one-third point from the left edge. Reserve this area and some space at the right margin to write notes to yourself at a later time. Don't worry about using more paper. The purpose of the extra space is to allow you room to revisit your notes and summarize, relate points to each other, clarify ideas that you had to skip over in class because you didn't have enough time, and give yourself ideas for improving your work. Because you come back to your notes outside of class, you can take the time to write neater, and you can use this "rewriting" as a way to review the lecture material. One of the key aspects of the Cornell method is to leave adequate space as you take notes so that you can insert comments later on.

Of course, you don't want to rewrite your notes word for word in the left column. Let your mind interpret what you've learned and write down only those essential points using single words or short phrases. You then have, on the right side of the paper, the notes you took in class along with the interpretive comments you inserted later; on the left side is your summary of these notes. You can use the left "summary" column when you're doing your weekly review and include the right "detail" column when studying for the exam.

One final point about notes: Try to exchange, or at least look over, notes with a friend to see if he or she took down something important that you missed. Looking at someone else's notes gives you another window into the lecture and helps give you a better comprehension of the material. Also, if you learn to take effective notes yourself, you probably won't have problems finding someone who is willing to swap notes with you.

# The "Chunk" Approach to Textbooks

Depending on the class, your textbook may be more or less important than your class notes. For some classes the textbook is mainly used to supplement the lecture. For others the text is the basis for the course, and lectures are used to clarify the reading. In either case, not learning all you can from the text is a mistake.

Many students read a textbook the way they would a novel. They start on page 1 and read until they finish the chapter. The problem with this approach is that textbooks are not novels. When you read a novel, the point is to follow the story line and be entertained. When you read a textbook, the point is to learn specific facts, skills, and definitions that will lead you to new insights. This different goal calls for a different approach.

The first task when reading a textbook is determining what you're supposed to learn in the chapter. The most obvious way to do this is by scanning the chapter to get oriented to the ideas, terms, and overall subject matter. Reading ahead may spoil the story in a novel, but it's definitely the best approach for reading a textbook. When you read ahead, concentrate most on the chapter's conclusion or summary. Typically, anywhere from 20 to 50 percent of the chapter's main points are contained in the summary. It stands to reason that if you have an idea about what the concepts are before you read about them in greater detail, you're ultimately going to learn them better.

The next step is to break down the chapter into specific chunks. The easiest way to do this is by using the various subheadings. However you break it up, consider that no chunk should be more than three to five pages long. Now each chunk becomes its own reading assignment. Don't try to read the entire chapter; in fact, don't even think about the chapter—just read the first chunk. For that matter, don't just read it—attack it. Give yourself a time limit to finish the first chunk (ten to fifteen minutes) and tell yourself that you must finish in that amount of time. With your pencil and highlighter in hand—go! Highlight key words, make short notes on important ideas, draw lines between ideas that relate to each other, and put question marks beside concepts that you don't understand. Devise your own system for making notes in the margins.

One caution about reading in chunks: Don't highlight or mark just anything; highlight only those key ideas that you'll want to refer to later. If in doubt, leave it out. Also, don't reread any portion of the chunk before you have read through it completely at least once. Your task is to finish the chunk within the time limit. If you finish it and decide you need to read some portion of it again, that's okay. But first finish the chunk and mark the important ideas.

When you finish the chunk, take a couple of minutes to review what you've done; look back at your notes and highlights and try to fix in your mind what you've learned. Take a short break (get a drink, take a walk down the hall) and then go on to the next chunk. When you finish the chapter, spend a few minutes reviewing the entire chapter and the summary again. Ask yourself: What do I know now that I didn't understand after I scanned the chapter the first time? Jot down these ideas, because they are probably some of the key points in the chapter.

After this, you're done with your reading! By reading in this manner, you'll find that you finish faster than if you tried to plow through the material from start to finish, and you'll avoid the most common problem students have with textbooks: staring at pages or passing your eyes over words for long periods of time without really reading or learning anything.

## Taking Control of Vocabulary

There is one more important point about reading. College professors use books that are at an advanced reading level. Sometimes even first-year students are confronted with readings that are really for more-advanced college students. Most first-year students encounter at least a few words they've never seen before in each reading assignment. Of course, you could just skip over the words, but one or more of those key words could end up on a test. Skipping words also causes you to lose comprehension of the entire reading assignment—the more you skip the more you don't understand. There's really no excuse for skipping words when a simple solution exists: Use a dictionary to look up words you don't understand and put them into a context. If Malcolm X could read the dictionary from cover to cover, you certainly can look up a few words. Sure, it's a hassle and it will slow you down; but the more words you look up now, the faster you'll read later and the more you'll learn. Your best bet is to keep a dictionary handy so that you can refer to it easily and move on with the assignment.

Here's an effective technique for dealing with new words: Buy a pack of three-by-five-inch index cards and a few strong rubber bands.

Active learning that involves interaction with others is far more effective than "going it alone."

When you encounter a word or phrase you don't understand—in a textbook, a lecture, or even in a discussion with a student or professor—jot it down on a card immediately. Look up its definition as soon as you can. On the card write the definition or explanation in language you can understand. Soon you'll have a set of key terms in the form of flash cards. An added bonus of the flash card system is that the cards can tell you a good deal of what you need to learn for exams. You may come to like note cards so well that you'll use them to take class notes. Limit your notation to one idea, fact, concept, or definition for each sequentially numbered card. After class, wrap a rubber band around the stack, making sure the date, course title, and specific topic are written on the top card. Some top-flight students do all their research and note-taking this way, even in graduate school.

## Two Heads Are Better Than One

One fundamental mistake that many students make is trying to go it alone. Research has shown that study groups are one of the most powerful tools for college success. And no wonder—study groups give you the power of several minds working on related problems. Instead of having to slog through twenty-five calculus problems on your own, a study group of five students could divide the assignment into five problems each. After each student works out her five problems, she can come back and teach them to the entire group. This method not only helps save time, but, when done properly, each person in the group learns more effectively. Because you have to teach some of the problems to others, you learn them more thoroughly yourself. You also know that you have a responsibility to the rest of the group—you had better know your stuff well or you'll really look bad. With problems that are especially difficult, the entire group can bear down and work on them together.

Of course, if you are the only student of color in a class, trying to form or get into a study group may be intimidating. Sometimes the best solution is to try to form study groups with other students of color who are taking the same class. If this idea is offensive to you, just remember that white students frequently form all-white study groups and don't think anything about it. It may require that you work on scheduling the same classes in the same sections with other students of color, but with some effort it can be accomplished, even if you encounter resistance. Remember again that white students don't give any thought to having classes composed of all or mostly all white students. Once you form a group and demonstrate its effectiveness, others will soon join in. Your adviser or minority student affairs office may be able to help you in this area.

## Proven Test-Taking Strategies: How to Finish with a Kick

At the end of the semester for most courses, you'll be asked to demonstrate your mastery of the material you covered in the class. For most students, final exams will be that demonstration. In introductory courses the most common testing method is the objective exam: true/false, fill in the blanks, multiple choice, matching, and so on. Many if not most college professors have had little if any training in test construction, so they may give answers away merely by the way the test is written. The following are some points to bear in mind before and during objective exams.

✔ Effective preparation for an exam involves your mind, body, and spirit. Avoid "all nighters" or heavy meals right before an exam. Light exercise an hour or so before an exam is a great way to focus and loosen up.

✔ Arrive about ten minutes before the exam—earlier than that and you may begin to get jumpy; later and you could be rushed.

✔ Read the directions carefully before jumping in. For example, "Choose the best response" does not mean the same thing as "Choose the correct response." By failing to carefully analyze the directions, you could be attempting to do something you're not being asked to do.

✔ After reading the directions, go through the entire exam, answering only those questions you're absolutely sure of. These questions are like money in the bank; if you run out of time, you may never get to questions that could have been answered easily. Remember, hard questions are often worth just as much as easy questions. Don't tackle the hard ones until after you've gotten the easy ones out of the way.

✔ After a first pass, answer those questions that require some thought, but that you are confident you can answer correctly. For these questions, quickly eliminate any responses you know are incorrect. Questions like this are the ones that usually have only two responses that you could intelligently choose from.

✔ Because students generally spend more time on questions on the first half of an exam, it can be a good idea to begin the second pass from the end of the exam and then finish at the beginning.

After you've answered the easiest questions on the test, you are left with questions you think the instructor got from the University of Mars. What do you do? Just guess wildly? Of course not. You now employ *intelligent guessing.* If you have no other way of figuring out the correct answer, do the following:

✔ Look for answers you know are incorrect or that you even think are incorrect and eliminate those as possibilities. Also eliminate answers that have gross errors in spelling, syntax, or grammar. Many times they are hastily written fillers.

✔ Look for patterns. Some test constructors are "B" or "All of the above" freaks. On some exams "All of the above" is correct virtually every time it is used. On most exams no clear pattern emerges immediately, but some have obvious patterns if you step back for a moment and look at all your answers at once.

✔ If you have no other way to tell, choose either the longest or shortest choice among the responses, whichever makes more sense.

✔ Answers that contain absolutes such as always or never are most often incorrect.

✔ Do not change your initial answer to questions. Two out of three times, you will end up with the wrong answer if you change it.

✔ Look at other parts of the test and see if the answer to your question is stated in another question or answer elsewhere on the test.

When nothing else works, you're running out of time, and you still have three or four unanswered questions, try the following:

✔ Try to determine what has been your most common choice and use it for all the remaining questions, or, failing that, choose C if the answer has four options or D if it has five options. These options are where instructors try to "bury" correct answers most often. Select one of these alternatives for all the remaining answers; do not vary or "shotgun" your responses. By doing this, you should get at least a few of the answers correct, even though you are only guessing.

One final note of caution: The test-taking techniques described here are obviously not foolproof, and they will not help much if you have not adequately prepared for an exam. You may also find that some professors know how to construct exams on which intelligent-guessing tips don't necessarily work. In such cases only excellent preparation will help you do well on an exam.

# Conclusion

This chapter just scratches the surface of learning the how-to's of academic success in college. The resources listed below can give you much more detailed information on improving your study skills. Your counselors, academic advisers, and professors can also give you lots of tips along the way. But the bottom line is this: Unless you decide to "just do it," no resource, whether a book or a person, will empower you to be your best. Only you can do that. And that's really what this chapter is all about. It's not for "weak" students any more than it is for "strong" students. All you can do is be your best, and it's in devotion to excellence that success in college begins.

# Resources

Ellis, Dave. *Becoming a Master Student,* 8th ed. (Boston: Houghton Mifflin, 1997).

Gardner, John N., and A. Jerome Jewler, eds. *Your College Experience: Strategies for Success* (Belmont, Calif.: Wadsworth, 1992).

# Chapter 4

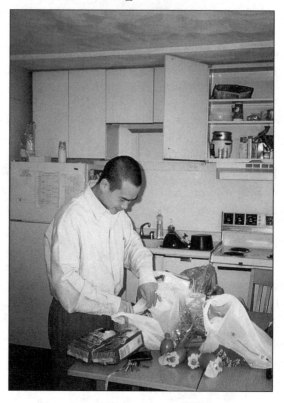

# To Your Health!

**Michael Blanco**

*Why am I always tired? I know I've been up half the night for three nights in a row, but I've done that before with no problem. Maybe you really can't eat pizza all week and feel okay. Or maybe it's because I've got three tests and a paper due next week and don't know how to squeeze it all in. I'm only eighteen now. If I keep going this way, what'll I feel like at thirty?*

It's great to be young. You feel good most of the time, your body usually works like a well-oiled machine, and it seems like there's nothing you can't do. Sure, you know you won't be young forever, but since you are now, you might as well enjoy the experience to the fullest.

Of course, it depends on what you mean by the "fullest." Hundreds of thousands of young lives have been permanently disabled or snuffed out because someone mixed a joy ride with alcohol. Illegal drugs, sexually transmitted diseases (STDs), and violence are other by-products of "fun" that destroy people with great potential. But even if you avoid these traps, you may be exposing yourself to other health risks that will affect you later in life. Other than the habits you establish early in childhood, nothing will influence your health choices so much as your habits in college. It is here where you develop new habits that affect many aspects of your life. Whether these habits are good or bad for your health depends on some decisions you will make during the four or five years of your college career.

## Health and People of Color

Although young people are typically thought of as being more healthy than middle-aged or elderly people, 20 percent of teenagers are differently abled or can be described as having some sort of illness. Unfortunately, this rate is even higher for people of color and in some regions is more than 50 percent. The primary causes of health-related problems for this group are teenage pregnancy, STDs, alcohol and drug abuse, and automobile accidents. As people of color get older, the level of health problems remains higher than for European Americans, and the primary problems begin to include such illnesses as heart disease, cancer, and diabetes. Of course, bad habits that are developed at a younger age, such as smoking and poor diet, affect these statistics greatly.

Stress is another factor that can affect your health as you get older. Racism and discrimination place people of color at greater risk for stress-related diseases. In general, people of color die at an earlier age and have to tolerate a lower standard of health throughout their lives than do European Americans. People of color also tend not to utilize institutional health care as frequently as European Americans because of language barriers, intimidation, mistrust of health-care providers, location of services, hours of operation, and finances.

Because college is a critical time in developing patterns that will affect the rest of your life, it can also be an opportunity to change the statistics back in your favor. Students who are healthy tend to get better grades and have a better overall college experience than those with poor health. By learning new health habits and by unlearning poor ones, you can be a better student now and ensure better health for your future.

## Starting on the Path to Better Health: Doing a "Health Inventory"

Complete the following "health inventory" by checking off items that describe your behaviors and lifestyle choices.

_____   I tend to eat fruits and vegetables more than sweets and fats.

_____   I am not sexually active, or I do have sex but always practice "safe sex" habits.

_____   I exercise regularly.

_____   I get at least six hours of sleep most nights.

_____   I don't smoke or use tobacco products.

_____   I don't use alcohol.

_____   I don't take illegal drugs.

_____   I don't drink and drive, and I refuse to ride when a driver has been drinking.

_____   I'm more concerned with avoiding a physical confrontation than protecting my reputation.

_____   I avoid situations I judge to be unsafe.

Obviously, the more items you check off, the stronger your health profile. The goal of this chapter is to help you improve this profile by adopting practices that can benefit your health for life.

## Health Concerns Among Ethnic Groups

It's important to know not only that people of color in general have different health concerns than European Americans—but also that differences exist among various ethnic groups. African Americans and

Hispanic Americans, for example, are much more at risk for AIDS than are Asian Americans and Native Americans; whereas Native Americans tend to have a higher rate of alcoholism than other people of color, and Asian Americans are more at risk for tuberculosis. Differences also exist within each group. For example, among Hispanics, Mexican Americans have higher rates of diabetes, and Puerto Ricans have a greater percentage of low-birth-weight infants. These differences are mostly due to where each group tends to live, health beliefs and practices, and social and economic status. For example, because AIDS has not yet become widespread on reservations, Native Americans who live there don't have as high a risk for the virus as African Americans who live in New York City.

To understand these differences further, it is useful to consider some of the primary health beliefs, practices, and concerns among respective ethnic groups.

### African Americans

Traditional African health beliefs and practices centered around oral history, medicine, and religion. Healers are an important part of African society, and their approach to health includes not only medicines, but spirituality, community, and family. In this regard African health is centuries ahead of Western medical practices. It is only within the past few years that American physicians have recognized the value of including more than just "science" in the practice of medicine, even though Africans have known this for centuries.

Despite these facts, African Americans suffer from many serious health problems. In addition to the high incidence of AIDS, major problems include high blood pressure, heart disease, diabetes, cancer, stroke, and infant mortality. Many diseases have causes that are directly linked to social problems within the African American community. These include teenage pregnancy, alcoholism, drug addiction, and depression. Life expectancy for African Americans is five years less than the norm, and twice as many African American children than children of European American descent die under the age of one.

### Asian Americans

Asian Americans tend to have a higher socioeconomic status than other people of color, and this factor has a positive effect on their health. Asian Americans do have special health concerns, however. Along with tuberculosis, hepatitis B is more common among Asian

Americans than other people of color, which may be due to contact with Asian countries where these diseases are still widespread. The greatest health hazard for Asian Americans, particularly men, is smoking. Smoking rates for Asian American men, depending on their country of origin, can be as high as 92 percent, compared with 30 percent among all Americans. Asian Americans are also prone to risk factors associated with public embarrassment and shame about health problems, which can occur when Asian Americans fail to live up to family or community expectations. These ideas are difficult to understand for those who are not Asian American, but they can cause a high degree of anxiety and depression. These problems can become worse, as some Asian Americans avoid medical treatment, especially for mental illnesses.

Asian health practices have traditionally centered around diet, herbs, and various forms of massage. Western medicine has long ignored the value of these treatments, but research has shown that some can be quite effective. Nevertheless, many Asian Americans now rely on Western medical practices and are the only group among people of color who are adequately represented in the medical profession.

## Hispanic Americans

As is true for many other people of color, the health of Hispanics/Latinos is related to poor economic conditions. Many Hispanics aren't able to pay to see a physician, or they may have difficulty getting to one. Many Hispanics are also poorly educated about health risks. These factors account for some of the major health problems among Hispanics. AIDS, for example, is up to eight times more common among some Puerto Rican groups than in the general population. Many Mexican American women are overweight compared with other Americans. Diabetes, liver disease, and accidental injuries are other problems among Hispanics.

Health practices among Hispanics vary, depending on what countries their families came from. People from South America have used traditional Western medical practices for many years. Mexican Americans, particularly from low-income backgrounds, drink teas and use herbs for treating illnesses, including mental illnesses. Religion is another important aspect for Hispanics. Most Hispanics are Christian, either Roman Catholic or Pentecostal. For Catholics, religious ceremonies may be central to their overall approach to health. Some

Pentecostals believe in a "health and wealth gospel," in which their health and finances are related to their devotion to their religion.

### Native Americans

Native Americans also believe that health is related to religion or spirituality. Traditional Native American beliefs view the world as a balance of many forces, both natural and supernatural. As part of this balance, Native Americans believe humans should fit into the world, not dominate it. Health occurs when harmony exists in the body, mind, and spirit. Illness is caused by a disharmony of these forces. Traditional Native American health practices seek to restore balance within a person. These practices include natural medicines and elaborate ceremonies, including the creation of beautiful works of art.

Since the invasion of the Americas by Europeans, Native Americans have suffered devastating diseases. Smallpox and other European diseases, for which Native Americans had no resistance, ravaged tribe after tribe. Europeans contributed to this holocaust by making gifts of blankets to tribes that were purposely contaminated with disease.

Native Americans continue to face many health challenges today. Unemployment and poverty are very high, and access to health care is often limited. Alcoholism, cirrhosis, diabetes, obesity, pneumonia, and accidental injuries are major health concerns among Native Americans.

# Health Risks in College

Many people think of college as a safe place, away from many of the problems of life. Depending on the college, this notion may have some truth. Most college campuses do have crime rates that are, in general, less than those of major cities. Most colleges also have some sort of health center that is staffed by at least a nurse, who can help students see a physician if they need to. Sometimes these centers even have mental health facilities and health education programs. Depending on the student and the college, a person may experience a better health environment in college than at home.

College life has its own share of health risks, however. Violence is increasing on college campuses, and places that were once considered safe are no longer so. College health centers usually don't have

Exercise is one of the keys to a healthy lifestyle.

enough staff to meet the demand and, unless it's an emergency, students may have to wait long periods to see a health-care provider (and precisely what constitutes an emergency is often a matter of opinion).

College life has its own unique health problems. Many of these problems can be associated with students who, perhaps for the first time, have to make important health decisions without the guidance of parents, teachers, church and community leaders, or extended family. Even if you've been on your own before college, the way others around you react to being independent for the first time can affect you. The following paragraphs identify some of the more common health concerns in college.

### Alcohol and Drug Abuse

Note the order of this category—alcohol, then drugs. Although often we think of illegal drugs as a more serious problem than alcohol, on college campuses alcohol is fast becoming the drug of choice. It's not difficult to understand why. Alcohol is more accepted in society than are illegal drugs. Underage drinking and public drunkenness have less severe laws attached to them than the use and possession of illegal drugs. College students tend to care about these differences because they hope to contribute to society one day. They know that a charge for possession of drugs will look a lot worse to a potential employer than an underage-drinking charge. In fact, in some professional circles that college students hope to one day be a part of, drinking is still regarded as acceptable and fashionable, so alcohol better fits into their future plans.

Another rationale is that most college students think that alcohol is safer than illegal drugs. This is not necessarily true and for society at large, alcohol poses a greater health risk. One of the problems is that it's harder to give out the "just say no" message with alcohol, because it is consumed at every level in our society, and most of that consumption is perfectly legal. Because of these factors, people can be lured into a false sense of security when it comes to alcohol.

For college students, this false sense of security typically comes out in binge drinking, with students drinking large amounts of alcohol at one time or getting drunk several days in a row. These kinds of practices have several immediate negative effects upon individuals. Alcohol prevents your brain from using its memory capacity to its fullest and hurts your athletic performance for up to 48 hours after you drink, even if you don't get drunk. Obviously, these problems are only made worse when you get drunk, especially if you do so on a regular basis. It's difficult enough to do well in college without drinking, so why make it tougher by trashing your body and pickling your brain?

Alcohol is especially deadly when you mix it with certain activities, such as driving and heavy partying. As mentioned already, automobile accidents and accidental injuries are special health concerns for people of color. Alcohol is often the culprit behind tragic accidents, both on and off the road. Some college students brag about how they get "smashed" or "wasted" at parties, but another side of this "fun," which especially affects women, is unprotected sex and rape. Alcohol impairs your judgment, and some people who would never engage in unprotected sex when they are sober will sleep with a stranger after a few drinks. A man who is drunk is more likely to rape a woman than if he were not, even if they are best friends. Thousands of college women who went beyond a few drinks have awakened in an unfamiliar bed to find their clothes scattered around the room. Often they have no memory of what happened after they passed out. AIDS and unwanted pregnancy are obvious health risks that make the tragedy of rape even worse. Sometimes even being around people who drink is dangerous. You can drink coffee and soda all night but still be killed or injured if you ride with someone who is drunk.

Drug use on college campuses today is actually on the decline. Of course, for those who regularly use most forms of illegal drugs, the health risks are greater than for alcohol. Unfortunately, the two drugs that have retained their popularity on campus are LSD and cocaine. These two drugs are very dangerous, but even a "safer" drug, such as marijuana, has major risks. Like alcohol, marijuana can impair your mental and physical abilities. Some students who detest cigarettes because of the cancer risk still smoke marijuana, even though it contains ten times more cancer-related chemicals than cigarettes.

## The Pleasure/Pain Roller Coaster

One of the greatest dangers with drug and alcohol abuse, of course, is dependency. Being dependent on alcohol or drugs can take several forms, from the weekend binge to full-blown addiction. Most people don't become dependent on drugs or alcohol after the first few times they use them, although, depending on the person and the drug, this possibility certainly exists. Some sort of progression into dependency usually occurs; if people spot this progression in time, they've got a lot better chance of not becoming addicted.

People usually take drugs or drink alcohol because it's fun or pleasurable to do so. For whatever reason, a normal state of mind is not good enough for those who abuse alcohol and use drugs. This idea explains why people of color can be prone to drug and alcohol abuse. Racism and discrimination, combined with poor economic conditions and even poor health, make the escape that alcohol and drugs provide attractive. The intoxication is therefore perceived as pleasurable compared with their experience without these substances. The first few encounters are experienced as moving from "normal" (which for some, might be quite painful) to an experience that is full of "pleasure." Of course, when the effects of drugs and alcohol wear off, the user returns to her or his former "normal" state, and usually somewhat worse for the wear and tear. This process is illustrated at the top of the next page.

Notice that before returning to "normal," depending on the substance being used, the person may experience more pain than before he or she began. With alcohol this experience is traditionally called a hangover. Of course, getting a hangover is usually not too bad if you had a lot of fun getting drunk, so the person may continue to drink despite this period of pain.

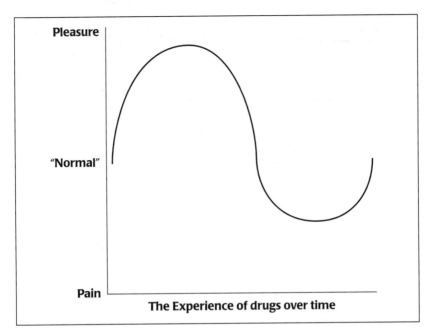

Pleasure

"Normal"

Pain

**The Experience of drugs over time**

Progress towards addiction, phase 1

As time goes on, however, and a person continues to abuse alcohol or drugs, this pattern changes. A person who is slipping into dependency will first notice that the pleasure—the "high"—associated with the use of these substances is not as great as it once was, and the pain is starting to increase; he or she may also notice that "normal" now seems more painful. When the person gets to this point, the "pleasure/pain roller coaster" starts to look different and begins and ends at different points, as illustrated at the top of the next page.

Notice that what the person experiences as "normal" is now somewhat painful. The experience does not provide as much pleasure as it once did, and the pain is now greater. Also notice that the amount of time a person experienced pain previously might be relatively small compared with the amount of pleasure. Now a person may feel pain longer than he or she feels high.

If a person finally sinks into addiction, the pattern changes again. Now "normal" is very painful, and the abused substance becomes a way of simply dulling the pain. Suicide is a real danger now, because the person is always in pain, and the effects of substance abuse distort reality. The person typically feels lost and without hope. This is illustrated at the bottom of the next page.

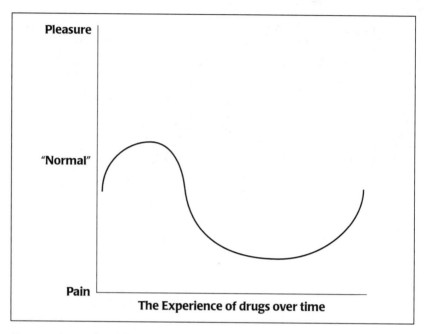

Progress towards addiction, phase 2

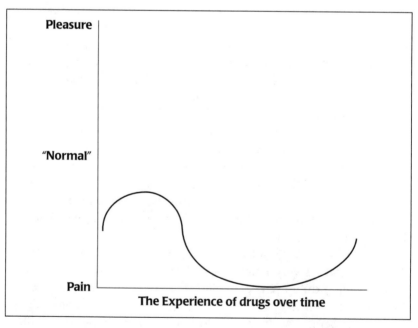

Progress towards addiction, phase 3

Of course, the best way to avoid this roller-coaster ride is to not use drugs or alcohol in the first place. Although drug abuse and alcoholism are diseases that can be affected by your genetic background, no one ever became addicted if they never used drugs or alcohol. If you drink or use drugs, however, it's important to be able to recognize these patterns. When you begin to experience some of the characteristics of the second pattern, it's time to get help. If you go to the third pattern, it will be much more difficult and expensive to return to a normal way of life.

# Sexuality and Sexually Transmitted Diseases

Another major health risk in college regards sexuality and sexually transmitted diseases (STDs). Some students who were not sexually active begin to have sex in college. Of course, some college students engaged in sexual intercourse before college but, as in other areas, the college environment is different and brings new risks. One risk regards safer sex practices. Some students of color from large cities who attend predominantly white institutions outside of a major city may think that they are at less risk for AIDS in their new environment and stop using condoms. Some students may begin to have different sexual partners and will continue to not use condoms. Of course, not using a condom is always a bad idea, but you increase your risk of STDs as you widen your circle of sexual partners. The point is, regardless of your sexual practices in high school, college is different and requires new levels of awareness and practice.

### Sexuality and Personal Values

Humans are sexual beings. Most people need sex, and many find abstinence to be an unrealistic or unwanted option. Some people find that sex at an early age or having sex with multiple partners satisfies their physical and emotional desires. For others, the best fulfillment of their needs is to have only one sex partner for life, whether by marriage or other permanent relationship. Of course, not everyone realizes their own ideal. People don't always find the right person, and many marriages end in divorce. People who want more sex partners can't always find them. Most people have to make some personal sexual adjustments, even those who are happily married. These adjustments can be healthy, depending on the circumstances and the needs of the individual.

Not all adjustments are healthy, however. The greatest danger lies in allowing other people's ideas regarding sexuality to be imposed upon you. This doesn't mean that you can't discuss your needs and values with others and use their ideas in developing your own set of beliefs and practices; but what works for others will not necessarily work for you. Sexuality, like other things in life, does not stand alone. Your family background, religion, social and economic environment, and other factors all play a role in your sexuality. Some people find that they must come to terms with a family experience that was less than ideal or a religious background that no longer works for them; for many people these influences have a positive role in their life.

The point is you should not allow your new college environment to impose values and practices upon you that don't fit you well. If you've decided that you don't want to engage in sex until later in life, you should feel good about this decision even if all your friends are sexually active. On the other hand, if your roommate comes from a more conservative background than you do and condemns your sexual practices, you will need to communicate that only you can determine your values and beliefs, not others.

## Sexuality as a "Disease"

As already mentioned, sexuality is a good and natural function of life, but it can become a form of disease if we use it to stunt our personal development and growth. Students of color at predominantly white institutions face circumstances that can lead to isolation and withdrawal. Although student communities composed mainly of students of color tend to be tightly knit, everyone does not necessarily fit in well. Some minority students gravitate to other student communities, including predominantly white ones, but other students find that they can relate to only a few other people on campus.

Some students substitute a sexual relationship with one other person for involvement in the broader community. Two students may decide to live together, go everywhere on campus together, and even study, do their laundry, and go shopping with each other—all at the expense of developing friendships with other students. In these cases, sexuality could become a way to cope with loneliness and feelings of isolation. Of course, not all people who live together do so for these reasons. Some people fall in love in young adulthood and successfully develop serious relationships. But many college students are not ready for this; they find that the relationship is simply an escape from problems they are experiencing. In these cases, students should seek advice from a minister, a counselor, or a faculty member they trust. They may find that they will ultimately do better to get out of these relationships and get involved in a larger circle of friends.

## The Threat of STDs

Of course, most college students know about AIDS, condoms, and sexually transmitted diseases (STDs). Millions of dollars have been spent on educating people about AIDS and STDs in the hope of stopping the spread of these diseases, and this education has not been in vain. Nevertheless, some people, even college students, remain ignorant about STDs and what they need to do to protect themselves. Education is not the final answer, however; your best defense is your own responsible behavior. Some people who are fully informed about the dangers of unsafe sex continue to behave in ways that increase their risk of AIDS. Some research indicates that condom use is going down, even among people who are well informed about AIDS. Simply knowing about AIDS and STDs won't protect you. Ultimately, the situations you find yourself in and the decisions you make about each situation will determine how well you protect yourself. Remember: Thousands of people who have made only one mistake now have AIDS.

Of course, AIDS is not the only STD that threatens you. Syphilis, chlamydia, gonorrhea, herpes, and venereal warts are epidemic on college campuses. Although none of these diseases is as serious as AIDS, some are incurable and can cause problems that will plague you for the rest of your life, such as recurring symptoms or permanent infertility. Remember that some college campuses that have a low incidence of AIDS may have a high incidence of other sexually transmitted diseases. Just because you're relatively "safe" from one disease doesn't mean you are from another.

## Protecting Yourself Against STDs

Of course, the only absolute protection from STDs is to not have sex at all. But for students who decide that this option is not for them, other approaches can be very effective. The most important weapon you have to protect yourself with is your own preparation for potentially dangerous situations. For example, if you go to a party without a condom, you are leaving yourself open for problems. The better you prepare yourself now, the less likely you'll do something you'll regret later. Here are some ways you can prepare yourself:

✔ Understand your values regarding sex and act in ways that are consistent with them. For example, if you have decided that you want to reduce the risk of AIDS by being sexually active with only one other person, you should be careful about how you go about developing relationships with others.

✔ If you are sexually active, always carry a latex condom with you—in fact, carry at least two. Condoms sometimes break during sex, and if you become aware of it and have another one, you can use it and increase the chances that you'll still be protected.

✔ Develop self-discipline in other areas, such as exercise.

✔ Limit your alcohol consumption, especially in unfamiliar situations. For example, if you are going to a frat party, determine that you won't drink until you become more familiar with the situation. Even when you are familiar with a specific environment, the less you drink, the safer you are.

✔ Practice answers to questions or arguments that are intended to convince you to do something you don't want to do. For example, if a man says, "I just can't feel good with a condom on," the partner might say, "And I can't feel good if I don't feel safe." Or, if a partner says, "Oh, let's not bother with a condom this time," you might say, "What I really don't want to bother with is sexually transmitted diseases. By using a condom, we're both protected from something that's far worse than a little 'bother.'"

### Take an STD Quiz

To increase your awareness about sexually transmitted diseases, take the following quiz by matching the disease with one of its characteristics.

1. Chlamydia        A. The most common STD among college students

2. AIDS        B. An incurable virus related to cold sores

3.  Venereal warts

4.  Gonorrhea

5.  Syphilis

6.  Herpes

C.  A potentially deadly disease that is most prevalent among heterosexual African Americans and women

D.  The most common STD in the United States

E.  A deadly, incurable disease caused by the HIV virus

F.  A bacterial infection that has developed strains that are resistant to antibiotics

*Answers: 1-D, 2-E, 3-A, 4-F, 5-C, 6-B*

To further your understanding of STDs, consider going to a health clinic and getting some literature on one or more of these diseases. If you have a sexual partner, consider discussing openly what you have learned about STDs and whether or not your practices should change accordingly.

# Health Opportunities in College

This chapter has thus far focused on the health risks associated with college, but college also presents a number of health opportunities. You will encounter new foods, educational opportunities related to your health, and facilities that allow you to explore new recreational activities.

### Food

Food can of course have a negative effect on your health, but in college you'll have an opportunity, perhaps for the first time, of determining your diet on your own. Many students gain weight significantly in their first year of college (a phenomenon commonly referred to as the "freshman fifteen"), so your choices in this area can have an immediate effect on your appearance, physical stamina, and wardrobe. If you live in a residence hall, which many colleges require for first-year students, your choices will be mostly limited to what is served at the dining halls; but most colleges, even smaller ones, have alternatives that are more healthy than traditional dorm food.

Eating "dorm" food typically calls for adjustments in eating habits.

In order to eat smart, always consider your options. Even if they're serving hot dogs and potato chips for lunch, they're probably also serving salad and a vegetable. And instead of three glasses of Mountain Dew, some orange juice or milk will ultimately give you more energy for your afternoon classes. In a pinch, peanut butter and jelly is a healthy alternative to other choices. In general, try to stick with cereals and grains (such as whole wheat bread and rice), and fruits and vegetables. Emphasize dairy products that are lower in fat, such as yogurt and skim milk rather than ice cream and whole milk. Fish, chicken, and meat are best when they are not fried, especially deep fried. Minimize foods that are high in fat and sugar. It's okay to get an ice-cream cone once in a while, but make it a special treat, not part of your daily routine.

## Health Education

College provides one of your best opportunities to enhance your education about your health. Especially in colleges with a Department of Health Education, a wide variety of courses on health education and nutrition exists, and many colleges require that students take at least one course in this area. If you take such a course, choose one that will ﹔st meet your own health needs. But bear in mind that you don't ｋ to take a college course to improve your health education. Many colleges have programs and workshops that focus on health-related issues, and most of these are free. You can keep up with these offerings by reading the college newspaper or asking about a calendar of events at the student union.

### Recreation and Personal Fitness

Most college campuses have at least adequate recreational and physical fitness opportunities, and many have facilities that rival the best fitness clubs—and at no cost. Don't limit yourself to sports you've played before. If you've never tried racquetball and your college has some courts, borrow a racquet from a friend and give it a whirl. Join an intramural team or a jogging club. Whatever you do, make sure you do it *consistently*. The main benefit of your exercise program is to learn habits that will stick with you for life. And don't overlook the value of walking. College students sometimes complain about having to walk here and there at large campuses. Some try to get rides or take a bus. But remember that walking three miles has many of the same benefits as running three miles. Incorporating walking into your overall exercise program can save you time and money.

## Conclusion

Good health is one of your most valuable assets in life. It can help you succeed in college, launch your career, nurture your family, and sustain you through the many stages of your life. Right now, good health may seem like something you can take for granted, but, unfortunately, you can't. You can destroy your health in minutes or protect it for decades. The choice is yours.

## Resources

Airhihenbuwa, Collins. *Health and Culture: Beyond the Western Paradigm.* Thousand Oaks, CA: Sage Publications, 1995.

Helman, Cecil G. *Culture, Health and Illness: An Introduction for Health Professionals,* 2nd ed. London: John Wright and Sons, 1990.

White, Evelyn C., ed. *The Black Woman's Health Book: Speaking for Ourselves.* Seattle: Seal Press, 1990.

# Chapter 5

here's a nasty name for everyon
EBE Spic Chink Savage JesusFreak
onky Polack Commie Dyke Dago W
o LIMEY Bitch Oreo Jap Coon Wetb
ntEyes Injun BibleBanger Spade Le
ok Boy Fairy Nazi Russki CamelJoc
itey OldGeezer TowelHead Kraut
dQueen UncleTom WASP Gimp JAPS
gleBunny Nigger OldBag Raghead
hWhore Kike Gringo Frog Tard Fag W

Including you.

THINK ABOUT IT.

# Racism on Campus

**Michael Blanco**

*Soon after this poster was distributed on a large university
campus several years ago, numbers of complaints were
registered about the "in your face" nature of the racial epithets.
The poster was withdrawn from circulation but ironically was
subsequently used on a number of other campuses around the
country and was the centerpiece of an MTV public service spot.*

**R**acism is one of the most important factors defining the history, culture, and existence of people of color in the United States, who have to learn how to deal with racism even from a very early age. Racism on campus puts some new faces on an old problem, however, and students need to learn how to most effectively deal with campus racism so that it doesn't prevent them from doing well in college.

# Defining Racism

Traditional dictionary definitions of *racism* usually associate it with beliefs regarding racial superiority. Racism is very complex, however, and these definitions leave out some of the most important dimensions of the practice.

### Prejudice and Racial Prejudice

Racism and prejudice are often thought of as the same thing. Although they are related ideas, racism and prejudice have significant differences. *Prejudice*, as the word implies, simply means making judgments about someone or something before having all the facts—the proverbial judging a book by its cover. For example, if you see someone driving an expensive car, you would probably assume that the person is rich or at least well off. This judgment may be true, but it's also possible that the person is a mechanic who is simply testing the car to make sure that it runs well after being repaired. In this sense, we can use our prejudices as mental short-cuts to help us get by in life without having to investigate all the details of our daily experiences.

Sometimes prejudices can be good and can even save our lives. If you were walking and came upon a large, barking dog that was chained up, you would be smart to prejudge that the dog was dangerous and stay away from it. Even if someone came by and told you that the dog wouldn't hurt you, it might still be wise to keep your distance. You would have good reason to discard your original prejudices only if the owner introduced you to the dog and showed you that it was friendly.

Of course, racial prejudice is different from the prejudices of our daily experiences. *Racial prejudice* converts reasonable fears into irrational phobia-based ignorance and brings forth the unfortunate human tendency to consider one group better than another. One definition of racial prejudice identifies it as a strong dislike or hatred of a person or group of persons based on incorrect and inflexible generalizations about their racial characteristics. According to this definition, anyone can be prejudiced against another person or group based on their race. Just as prejudice and racial prejudice are different, however, racism goes beyond racial prejudice by including another unfortunate human characteristic—the use of power against others.

## Racism and Power

Many sociologists indicate that racism comes about when power is applied against people using racial prejudice as the justification. This power can be exerted by individual people or entire institutions, such as school districts or even federal and state governments. Further, racism may be intentional or unintentional and may even have the support of an entire culture. American history is perhaps the best example of this idea. Within 150 years after the Europeans arrived in North America, indigenous American Indian populations had been reduced to a fraction of what they once were, and a legal institution existed that allowed for the total subjection of African slave labor.

Unfortunately, despite the many changes in the legal status of African and Native American people, they still have little economic or political power compared with whites. Accordingly, including power in a definition raises an interesting question: Can people of color in America exert racism against whites? Since the power structures of our society are still controlled by people who are primarily of white European ancestry, how can people of color be racist in any sort of meaningful way? People of color can be just as prejudiced as white people can, but it is difficult to imagine them exerting racism when whites dominate the power structures of the United States. This is not to suggest that racial prejudice is somehow "better" than racism; however, the *effect* of racial prejudice is considerably different, depending on who exerts it and who receives it because of the power differential that exists between different groups. The effects of racial prejudice have had little effect on the dominant group in American society, whereas racism has had a devastating effect on people of color in America.

Of course, race is not the only variable that people can use against others. Throughout history, groups in power have attempted to exploit weaker groups based on differences in language, religion, and culture. People can learn new languages, change their religion, and adapt to different cultures, but because racial differences can usually be readily seen and do not change throughout successive generations, people of color remain an easy target for the dominant group.

# Racism on Campus

College campuses are places where racism should not exist. Colleges are oases of knowledge and critical thinking, and racism is a product of ignorance and irrationality. One hopes that college is a place that encourages people to examine what stands behind their hatreds and prejudices, and that they would abandon them in favor of tolerance and equality. Unfortunately, what should be is not what actually is. In order to understand why, we need to understand the complex make-up of racism on college campuses.

## Ignorance on Campus

One dangerous misconception about college students, professors, and administrators is that they are "educated," whereas those without college degrees are not. Obviously, people with college degrees, especially those with advanced degrees, have expertise in their given field of study, although the explosion of knowledge over the past one hundred years has radically affected what having a college education means. Hundreds of years ago, it was possible for someone to gain a mastery of the major branches of knowledge that they were presented within their various cultures. Phyllis Wheatley, Tecumseh, Eugenio María de Hostos, K'ung Su-Tse, and Benjamin Banneker are examples of people who did this.

Knowledge today has become so voluminous and specialized that no one person is able to understand even the basics of all the major fields of study. Many white college students and professors are ignorant of the major issues that confront people of color today. For example, most college professors regard the way students of color use English as substandard to English as spoken by most white Americans. Linguists understand that "Black English" and other ethnic dialects are as legitimate as "White English," but because most professors remain ignorant of this fact, they assume that some students of color are deficient in their ability to express themselves verbally.

Whereas ignorance regarding these issues is key to their survival, as noted previously, power is a crucial component of racism. Just as other large institutions employ power to accomplish their goals, colleges and universities use power for their own ends and to promote ideas and programs that they support.

## Power on Campus

Colleges have long traditions of educating the elite and powerful. Although many colleges talk about reaching out to the less fortunate, the power structures of most schools still mainly support the upper crust of society. In fact, minority scholarships are quite controversial in higher education today because of their cost, even though millions of dollars more are spent on merit scholarships, which continue to elude most groups composed of people of color. The dominant group has set up the rules so that those who receive the greatest educational privileges and best understand the language of higher education (i.e., as judged by their ability to do well on standardized tests) get most of the educational benefits. Yet recent court decisions have targeted the small amount of money given for race-based scholarships as discrimination.

One reason for this inequity is that dominant groups tend to take care of themselves at the expense of others. This fact explains why racism continues to exist alongside the great wealth of knowledge on college campuses. People may "know better," but they also don't want to give up privileges that work to their advantage.

Of course, students are as concerned about power as institutions are. As higher education has become more expensive, students in the dominant group have become more angry about all the so-called advantages that students of color have. Many myths, such as "minorities are here on a free ride," persist on many college campuses today. This anger causes these students to strike out at students of color, and research indicates that racial incidents are on the rise on college campuses today.

Students from the dominant group also use another myth—reverse discrimination—to support their ideas and justify their actions. They refuse to see that it is impossible for a group with little or no power to discriminate in any kind of meaningful way against a group that holds the vast majority of power. People who have power get so used to it that they delude themselves about how much power they really have and how they use it against the powerless. Whites may cite the "great melting pot" analogy of America as a land of equity, but they fail to recognize that many people of color didn't melt, partly because they didn't want to melt, and partly because whites refused to let them melt.

## "Unintentional" Racism

Not all racism comes from a conscious decision by a person or group to use power against others. Sometimes people and institutions are so used to the power structures that work for them that they "unintentionally" buy into ideas that work against others. One example already mentioned regards the use of standardized test scores (SATs or ACTs) to determine college admission. Many researchers have concluded that standardized test scores have less value than they are credited with in predicting success in college, especially among students of color. Many argue that standardized tests are biased toward white students because they reflect the values and culture of white America. Students of color who do poorly on standardized tests can do well in college, even at predominantly white institutions, because they have an opportunity to adapt to the white environment of the college long before they graduate. These same students, however, obviously do not have this kind of opportunity during the short time they have to complete a standardized test. Ultimately, students of color can be just as or more successful than white students, even if they initially have lower test scores.

Despite these facts many colleges and universities still place a heavy emphasis on standardized tests because, in part, higher SAT or ACT scores among an institution's students enhance its prestige and national rank. Of course, most colleges and universities will tell you that they use SAT or ACT scores to ensure that they admit students who can succeed and to enhance the academic quality of the institution. What these schools often fail to recognize is that diversifying the academic community of an institution also improves academic quality. By placing too much weight on standardized test scores, institutions can create an academic environment that is more uniform and sterile than it otherwise could be.

The point in discussing unintentional racism is not to relieve the stigma of racism because it is unintentional. Many people and institutions use justifications and rationalizations to mask racism that is very intentional. But, ultimately, it doesn't really make much difference if people or institutions *intend* to be racist or not. If the *impact* of decisions or policies is racist, the intent is of secondary importance. Unintentional racism needs to be criticized as harshly as intentional racism. In fact, unintentional racism may need to be criticized more harshly, because it probably does more harm. Powerful people and institutions do not want to appear intentionally racist, so they couch their racism in policies that, despite the "equal opportunity" label, continue to favor the privileged. These policies continue to have damaging effects for people of color, perhaps even more damaging than those that are caused by intentional racism. It's a hollow victory to be able to sit on any seat on the bus if you don't have a decent paying job to ride to.

# Dealing with Racism

Throughout America's history people of color have shown great resilience and determination in dealing with racism. Despite the best attempts to marginalize and even eliminate them, people of color have risen to the top in every period of American history. Their story is one of a proud struggle against the worst odds; at some points in history, depending on the measures used, people of color have shown higher standards of living than white Americans. For example, until recently the suicide rate was lower among African Americans than for white Americans.

Nevertheless, for the most part, the effects of oppression against people of color have taken a terrible toll. Despite the increasing so-called freedoms that they now have compared with the past, in some of the most important areas that mark true equality people of color are actually losing ground. People of color continue to lag well behind white Americans in terms of education, economic status, health care, and other important measures of social standing. Some institutions, such as the family and church, have played a significant role in reducing the negative effects of poverty, poor education, and inadequate health care. But these institutions cannot be expected to counter all of the problems that people of color face, and some of these institutions now appear to be overwhelmed by a task that grows ever larger. Soaring crime rates, increased drug and alcohol abuse, single-parent families, and other problems are the results of communities that are under attack from our society.

## Racism and Anger

Perhaps the most common response to racism is anger. Anger is a natural outgrowth of racism and can be very destructive, especially when combined with hopelessness and hatred, including self-hatred. Suicide, murder, drug addiction, alcoholism, and many other social problems are the results of anger, hopelessness, and hatred.

Anger can also be a positive force, however. If people can maintain hope and love, including self-love, they can use anger to accomplish incredible feats that make positive contributions to their communities, our nation, and even the world. Anger prompted Martin Luther King, Jr. to initiate the Montgomery bus boycott, and it motivated Cesar Chavez to organize migrant farm workers to protest against poor wages and working conditions. The big question is why some people use anger to destroy and others use it to effect positive change.

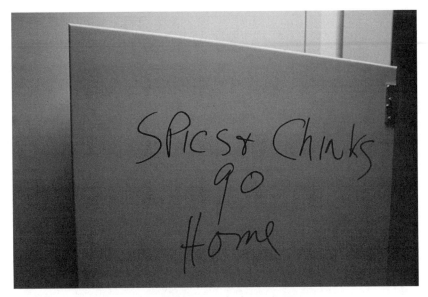

In spite of education and efforts at sensitization, racism still exists—and to many remains this country's number one social problem.

## Racial Identity Development

Several researchers, including some prominent people of color, have examined the psychological dynamics of racism and have concluded that people go through four stages in dealing with it. People tend to express anger and other feelings about racism based on where they are in these developmental stages. The ideal is to progress to the last stage, where a person attains inner strength and harmony despite racism in society, and anger regarding racism is channeled into positive action that promotes sustained efforts to fight it without resorting to behaviors that are ultimately self-destructive. Although researchers have debated the finer points of racial identity development, and individual racial and ethnic groups have their own specific issues associated with their experiences of racism, four basic stages have emerged that describe how people of color deal with racism.

### Stage One: Lack of Critical Awareness
The first stage of dealing with racism for most people of color involves a lack of critical awareness regarding racism. At this stage people of color may attempt to minimize racial differences or even try to identify with the dominant white culture. Some people may even deny their

own racial identity in an attempt to "be white." People at this stage may be very naive about race or attempt to pass off issues regarding race as being unimportant. When taken to the extreme, some may exhibit a kind of racism toward people in their own racial or ethnic group.

As can be imagined, people in this stage do not tend to feel very good about themselves. As much as they might try, they cannot "be white," and they cannot deny that race is very important in our society. Sooner or later their increasing awareness about the importance of race and how it affects their lives brings about an onslaught of self-doubt, which can soon turn into self-hatred. If they remain in this stage, anxiety, depression, and social and family problems will often come about. Although many people in this stage are children and adolescents, some adult individuals never gain a critical awareness of racism and live their lives in the psychological shadow of the dominant white culture.

### Stage Two: Increasing Critical Awareness and Search for Self-identity

When a person of color learns that he or she cannot nor should not simply fit into white culture and begins a search for self-identity within his or her own racial framework, a transition is made to the second stage. In stage two people begin to find out who they are and they start to gain an appreciation of their own culture apart from white culture. People in this stage experience both positive and negative feelings about themselves. On the one hand, an increasing awareness of self and one's culture leads to more positive self-esteem but, on the other hand, this stage can also be very confusing. As people become more positive toward their own group, they often experience negative feelings toward the dominant group. How people handle these conflicting feelings influences their own personal framework.

### Stage Three: Total Transfer to One's Own Culture

Once people of color find their identity within their own racial or ethnic group, they often transfer all of their feelings and loyalties to that group at the expense of all other racial or ethnic groups. Not only do they believe that their culture is good, they believe that other cultures, especially the white establishment, are inferior to their own. People in this stage are very angry about the oppression they have experienced, and sometimes they seek out means of striking back at their oppressors. Although one might imagine that this stage is characterized by higher self-esteem, much research has found lower self-esteem and feelings of inferiority among people in stage three. Other problems include higher levels of anxiety, less mature personal relationships, and concerns about drug abuse. It appears that the intense anger associated with this stage has negative effects on the people who are in it, despite their newfound personal and cultural identities.

### Stage Four: Balance and Social Responsibility

Ultimately, some people in stage three recognize that no one culture is perfect and that all cultures have both negative and positive characteristics. In stage four people develop a more balanced sense of how they fit into their own culture and other cultures. People in this stage retain their pride about their own race and culture, but they also come to appreciate the contributions of other races and cultures. They also begin to see how people from all racial and ethnic groups can cooperate to improve society. People in this stage often develop a strong sense of their own social responsibility and direct their anger toward positive channels of change. Some research regarding people in stage four has found higher levels of self-esteem and psychological adjustment, which may be due to less intense feelings of anger associated with this stage.

The value of racial identity development is to give people of color a tool to use in dealing with anger. When Martin Luther King, Jr. said, "I have a dream," his dream reflected a person who had learned to progress through his anger and use it in a positive way, as is characterized by stage four. As people of color identify with the various stages and understand how they can relate to them, they improve their chances for using their own anger in a positive way. Although racial identity development is not a cure-all for the psychological and social problems associated with racism, it can help people understand their attitudes and behaviors and prompt them to make positive changes.

# Exercise on Racial Identity Development

Read the following statements and questions and indicate the stage (one, two, three, or four, based on the preceding discussion) that best characterizes it. Share your answers with others and discuss why you gave the answer you did. Although some statements or questions may seem obvious, it should be remembered that all are subject to various interpretations, and some are intentionally ambiguous to promote careful thinking.

| Statement/Question | Stage |
|---|---|
| I can't believe white people are so ignorant. | _____ |
| Historically, white people have caused more harm to the world than any other racial group. | _____ |
| We've all got to work together to make things better. | _____ |
| I just wonder who I really am. | _____ |
| We've brought all these problems on ourselves. | _____ |
| "Red, Brown, Yellow, Black and White, we are precious in His sight." | _____ |
| Why can't you just try to fit in and not make trouble? | _____ |
| I'm not going to hate whites, because it ultimately ends up hurting me. | _____ |
| Why do all Barbie dolls have blond hair? | _____ |
| People of color are people of the sun; white people are people of the ice. | _____ |

Continue this exercise by making some statements about racial issues that you consider to be true, or ask some questions about race. After each question, make an evaluation of what stage the statement or question best fits into. The purpose of this exercise is not for you to put yourself or others into any one category, but to examine your own attitudes and development regarding race.

# White Identity Development

While most people of color can understand the model of racial identity development presented in this chapter, it is also important to recognize that whites also go through a similar process regarding their race and the advantages they have in society because of it.

### Stage One: Lack of Critical Awareness

Just as people of color are initially unaware of dimensions regarding race in our society, so also are whites. At this stage whites are not aware of the privileges they enjoy because they are white; or if they do have some awareness, they tend to regard it as unimportant or as the way things ought to be. Whites in this stage do not believe that they or their culture has oppressed people of color, and they accept the common stereotypes regarding people of color. Obviously, many whites, especially those who live in areas that have few people of color, remain in this stage for life and are content with their place within the dominant culture. Accordingly, no psychological problems are associated with this stage, since the personal self-esteem of whites in this stage is reinforced by white dominance in society.

### Stage Two: Increasing Awareness and "White Guilt"

Those whites that move beyond mere acceptance of a white-dominated society do so because of an increasing awareness of the privileges they enjoy because they are white and how American society has oppressed people of color. Whites in this stage experience a conflict over the desire to remain comfortable in a world where they have the upper hand and the overwhelming evidence that their comfort relies upon the oppression of people of color. Whites in this stage experience guilt, depression, and a decrease in self-esteem.

### Stage Three: Antiracism or Retreat into White Culture

Whites who move into stage three have wrestled with the issue of racism and have decided to either step out into the fight against it or retreat into the safety of white dominance. Whites who decide to oppose and fight racism may become militant and even anti-white, though this is rare; John Brown and William Lloyd Garrison can be viewed in this light. Individuals in this stage may experience guilt and self-anger over their previous acceptance of white culture. Whites who decide to retreat into white culture may initially attempt to fight racism, but they soon find this option difficult to sustain and decide it is not worth the effort. They may be confronted by other whites, who see them as "pro-minority," or by distrusting people of color, who question the sincerity of their support. These people may ultimately become vehemently pro-white and develop extreme fear and hatred of people of color. This fact explains why people of color are suspicious of whites who are "antiracist," since they know these whites may ultimately hurt them worse than whites who never move into stage three.

### Stage Four: Balance and Redefinition

Whites in stage three who do not retreat into white culture become candidates to move into stage four, which is characterized by balance and redefinition. Whites in this stage come to accept their whiteness despite its negative history and associations. Whites in this stage acknowledge their own continuing racism, and they often attempt to educate themselves in a desire to uncover their own prejudices that they still may be unaware of. They are still socially active against racism, but their energy may be redirected toward other forms of oppression as well. Whites in this stage may still experience some "white guilt," but it is less pronounced than in stages two and three.

In comparing racial identity development of whites and of people of color, at least one important fact stands out: People of color have strong motives to learn to deal with racism since racism affects them so negatively. Very few people of color remain in stage one, and most progress to either stage three or stage four. On the other hand, white people have no strong motivation to go beyond stage one, which is a comfortable place to be. All that whites need to do is block out reality well enough and stay in their white cocoon. Therefore, although people of color need to be aware of their own progress through different stages, they must also realize that many if not most whites do not make the same effort. Although this realization may cause people of color further anger, as yet another example of how they must work harder than whites in our society, it also helps to explain the criticism that "white people are so ignorant." White people are ignorant when it comes to issues of race because they have little motivation to become educated. This fact does not excuse whites from progressing to stage four, but people of color need to at least appreciate this aspect of white identity development so that they can better deal with white racial ignorance.

## Dealing with Racism on Campus on a Personal, Individual Level

Although racial identity development provides people of color with a good basis for dealing with racism in general, racism on campus has its own particular wrinkles. How do you deal with the professor who thinks you don't belong in college because you're a "minority admit"? Or what about the person in financial aid who seems to be able to help just about everyone else in line except you? And yes, at a predominantly white institution, you'll probably have to deal with at least one situation that involves blatant racism against you personally.

## Go to Class!

Nikki Giovanni, a prominent African American educator, in her article "Campus Racism 101," gives several suggestions for dealing with racism at predominantly white colleges and universities. Among these suggestions are three key practices: go to class, meet your professors, and do assignments on time.

Dr. Giovanni's suggestions are based on some important ideas. People of color at predominantly white institutions, for the most part, do not have the advantage of remaining "invisible" to their professors or other students. If you're the only African American in your class, even if it is a large class, people will notice you, including your professor. If you don't come to class for a week, your professor and some of your classmates will probably take note. Or, if you come to class but read the newspaper or put up your feet while you listen to music on your Walkman, you're going to send an equally negative message. On the other hand, if you're there every class period, sitting up front and participating, you'll send a completely different message. Your behavior will either reinforce or contradict negative stereotypes associated with people of color, however unfair those stereotypes are. And stereotypes not only affect how people respond to you personally, they may even determine your grade in a class. Don't expect professors to give you the benefit of the doubt where your grade is concerned if you haven't taken their classes as seriously as you should have. Attendance is key.

As important as other people's perceptions are, your own perception of yourself is your primary defense against racism on campus. Obviously, even your best efforts will not be rewarded with an environment that is free of racism. But racism has the most negative effect on those whose view of themselves supports racist stereotypes. People of color are often plagued by self-doubt, especially regarding academics. Racism hurts most when students of color believe the lie that they're not as capable and talented, or that they don't really deserve to be at a prominent college or university. Positive academic behavior supports a positive view of yourself and your place within a predominantly white institution. You must believe that if you do what you should to succeed, you will succeed. You must also refuse to follow the example of students who don't take college seriously, even if it appears to be cool or "the thing to do."

Another rationalization for not working hard is that the professors are racist. Many professors are racist, and you may have to work harder to get the grades you deserve. But giving up hurts only you, not the professor. And not working your hardest will only weaken your own self-image regarding your ability to compete and be successful, which ultimately makes you even more vulnerable to racism.

## See the Big Picture

Many students come to college to prepare for a well-paying job. And though college is certainly a good place to prepare for careers that have high salaries, some students avoid taking courses outside their vocational interests, or do so only because they have to. Students who take this approach are cheating themselves of knowledge of subjects that are crucial to understanding racism and other problems in our society. Not only are courses in ethnic studies valuable, but courses in history, women's studies, sociology, psychology, anthropology, and other areas can broaden your perspective on life and social issues. Some research indicates that students with a strong background in the liberal arts perform better in some job fields than students who had training only in the area in which they end up working. A comprehensive educational experience will not only better equip you to deal with campus racism, it will better prepare you for your career and adult life.

## Get Involved!

Learning in college is not limited to the classroom. College is a total educational experience that affects students' attitudes, values, and entire orientation to life. To take advantage of all that college offers, students need to become involved in many facets of college life. Virtually all colleges have co-curricular activities, such as clubs, professional organizations, sororities and fraternities, student government, and interest groups. If you plan to become an engineer, join an engineering club. Get on the staff of the student newspaper, even if you're not a journalism or English major. These activities will increase your visibility on campus as a mover and a shaker and will bolster your own confidence about your standing within the institution. This confidence will increase your ability to deal with racism when you encounter it. Not only will you know about more resources on campus to fight racism, but you'll feel more committed to combating it and will have more confidence in your ability to make a difference.

A vital component in fighting racism on campus is the clubs and organizations that are devoted to supporting people of color and promoting issues of concern to them. Such groups may be given names

Public demonstrations supporting antiracism programs are appearing at PWIs with some frequency.

like "Native American Association," "Black Caucus," "Asian American Coalition," or "Hispanic/Latino Club." Depending on the size of the institution, organizations such as these may be grouped into a single "Multicultural Association," or may exist side-by-side with a more inclusive group. Involvement in organizations such as these has a positive influence on students of color. In addition to finding a supportive community in these groups, they can band together to promote positive change on campus. Many of the changes in higher education have come about through student activism, and clubs and organizations are usually behind most student movements to reform higher education. Determine that you will not passively accept the way things are on campus, but that you will be an active promoter of change by grouping together with others who share similar concerns and interests.

## Conclusion

This chapter has provided some tools for helping you deal with racism as you go through college. The perspectives presented here are important because racism is one of the major reasons students of color do not succeed in college. In this sense, how students of color deal with racism can radically affect them, since graduating from college is one of the most important factors in many people's lives. Dealing with racism ultimately cannot be limited to college, however. As with many things, coping with racism is a lifelong experience, and those who prepare to consistently educate themselves about racism stand a much better chance of making lasting changes for themselves and society. College should be your first step in a life that is at least partially devoted to ending racism in the world.

# Reference

Giovanni, Nikki. "Campus Racism 101" (*Essence,* August 1991), pp. 71–72.

# Resources

Helms, Janet E. *A Race Is a Nice Thing to Have: A Guide to Being a White Person or Understanding the White Person in Your Life* (Topeka: Content Communications, 1992).

Ponterotto, Joseph G., and Paul B. Pedersen. *Preventing Prejudice: A Guide for Counselors and Educators.* Multicultural Aspects of Counseling Series 2, Paul Pedersen, ed. (Newbury Park, Calif.: Sage Publications, 1993).

Sidel, Ruth. *Battling Bias: The Struggle for Identity and Community on College Campuses* (Newbury Park, Calif.: Sage Publications, 1993).

West, Cornell. *Race Matters* (Boston: Beacon Press, 1993).

# Chapter 6

# Ethics and Moral Decision Making

**Michael Blanco**

*Professor:  There are no absolutes.*

*Student:  Are you sure?*

*Professor:  Absolutely!*

Talking about ethics is like talking about global politics. Everyone has an opinion, and many employ good reasoning to back up their ideas. The problem is that others employ good reasoning to support viewpoints that are very different from ours. Even if we are certain that our way of thinking is correct, it's hard to prove it to someone else who's just as knowledgeable and opinionated. So it's tempting to avoid discussions of ethics altogether. We all know what's right for us, so what else really matters? Besides, what do ethics have to do with college, anyway?

Unfortunately, it's not that simple. Ethics are personal, yes, but they involve our interactions with others. For a devoted environmentalist who conscientiously reuses paper clips, it's frustrating to see others tossing soda cans into a trash can that's sitting right next to a recycling bin. Issues such as war, nuclear power, gay rights, and abortion exist because of conflicts in ethical values among individuals, groups, and nations. Ethics are important for students because college brings together diverse people who interact about ideas. And because many college students live together, differences in viewpoints often end up on your doorstep. The issues are more complex than your liking a clean room while your roommate doesn't know where the laundry basket is. Diversity in such things as religion, sexual norms, and attitudes toward authority can lead to severe conflicts. How you handle differences between your viewpoints and those of others is as important as the viewpoints themselves.

## Understanding Ethical Viewpoints

Most people understand where their ideas on ethics come from: parents, religion, law, education. Often we believe that the experiences of others are similar to our own, so much so that we believe that others somehow *ought* to think the way we do about certain issues. This approach may work for people in small, close-knit communities, but it won't work for those in large, public universities or even most colleges. And sometimes people agree on something for very different reasons. For example, two people may agree that sex outside of marriage is wrong; one may base this on religious beliefs or personal values, however, whereas another may ground it in the threat of sexually transmitted diseases. This example points to a profound difference in how people approach ethics. For some, ethics are grounded in eternal principles that govern the universe. Religion and belief systems that appeal to a higher power usually view ethics in this light. For others, ethics refer to conduct that will produce the best results for everyone. Most people combine these beliefs in some manner, but they do so in different ways. These differences often lead to conflicts that come as much from our not understanding the *basis* of another person's position as from disagreements over the issue itself.

# Morals, Ethics, and Values

Although no formula exists for understanding how people define ethics, generally speaking, people use three different approaches, depending on the circumstances, for gauging right from wrong. For convenience, this chapter employs the terms *morals, ethics,* and *values* to describe these approaches.

Of course, one of the dangers of using terms to identify different approaches to ethics is that some people may use them to label others as unethical or immoral. Very few people deserve such a label. It is much better to describe actions rather than people as immoral or unethical, and even this approach has problems. Also, in most discussions on ethics these terms are used interchangeably, even by philosophers and theologians, so you should be careful about drawing sharp distinctions between them. The value of these terms as they are used here is to underscore the differences in the way people approach ethics, but you should avoid using them in a way that would label others or indicate too sharp a distinction in a general discussion on ethics.

### God and Religion: Morals

Theologians refer to *moral theology* as the aspect of religion that describes God's moral principles for the world. Typically, these rules are universal, absolute, and unchangeable. Because the authority for these laws is a divine being (or beings) who is, by definition, far above humanity in terms of power, wisdom, and justice, humans have no basis to question or change them, regardless of the circumstances. This type of approach can be characterized as emphasizing the moral dimension of right and wrong. It is immoral to steal or harm someone because it violates God's moral will. Obviously, many if not most of the major religions of the world hold this view.

Other religions take a moral view of right and wrong based on transcendental laws of the universe. This idea is similar to moral theology because it also emphasizes that morals are permanent and come from a source outside of humanity, but this view does not necessarily maintain that a personal God rules the universe. Under this view it is always wrong to violate moral laws because they govern the entire universe for all time.

## The Common Good for Humanity: Ethics

As opposed to morals, *ethics* highlight the common good for humanity rather than God's divine rule. People who approach right and wrong based on ethics are not necessarily atheists or agnostics; but if they believe in God, they emphasize that God's primary moral intent is for humans to attain the greatest common good or happiness. Murder is wrong not so much because it offends God but because it contributes to human misery. Under this view ethics may change as circumstances change. For example, before the nuclear age, world war might have been regarded as a necessary evil to suppress a powerful tyrant, such as Hitler. Today the moral imperative to solve national conflicts using peaceful means is much more urgent.

People who emphasize morals over ethics do not necessarily deny the importance of human happiness, rather they tend to believe that human happiness is attained by following God's rule, even if God's law appears to be repressive or undemocratic. By contrast, people who emphasize ethics over morals tend to define God's morals by what appears to be best for all humanity.

## Personal Preference and Opinions: Values

Regardless of his or her position on morals or ethics, everyone has values. Values do not so much emphasize right and wrong as likes and dislikes. One person likes Cajun food while another likes meat and potatoes. Music, clothing, politics, and many other areas are subject to different values that individuals place on them. Differences in values can bring about as much conflict as moral or ethical differences. Some people may not attach any negative moral or ethical significance to rap music, for example, but they may nevertheless hate to listen to it. In other words, they may not think it is wrong to listen to rap music but may dislike your playing it in their presence. If such a person is your roommate and you like to listen to loud rap music, the results can be disastrous to your relationship. Political opinions are another hot button. Most Democrats don't think it is morally or ethically wrong to be a Republican, but they might contend it is wrongheaded. In order to live cooperatively in an environment that has a diversity of viewpoints, one must always consider the place of values and opinions along with morals and ethics.

## Exercise on Morals, Ethics, and Values

Look over the following statements and indicate agreement (A) or disagreement (D) in the column before each statement. In the space following the statement, indicate the basis on which you made your response; for example, religion, parents, rules, law, or common sense. Finally, categorize your response as based on morals, ethics, or values, by writing *M, E,* or *V,* respectively, after each answer.

_____ It is *always* wrong to tell a lie.

_____

_____ It's okay to copy from someone else's test.

_____

_____ You shouldn't drink alcohol and drive.

_____

_____ Homosexuality is a sin.

_____

_____ Homosexuality is wrong.

_____

_____ You shouldn't pick up a hitchhiker.

_____

_____ All eligible voters should vote.

_____

_____ Bracelets that can monitor the whereabouts of convicted, nonviolent felons should be used.

_____

# Navigating Among Diverse Ethical Viewpoints

Understanding different ethical viewpoints is only the first step in successfully relating your own to others in your community. The purpose of recognizing diversity in ethical viewpoints and approaches is *not* to water down your own convictions and beliefs—society needs individuals with strong moral and ethical vision. Without a moral vision, Martin Luther King, Jr. would have simply been another Baptist pastor. Although his vision of justice was clearly rooted in Christian principles, he was broad enough in his appeal to work with people from all religious or non-religious persuasions, even though their ideas about ethics might be different from his. Conversely, he was quick to point out the hypocrisy of those who called themselves Christians and still advocated discrimination and prejudice.

Dr. King's method for attaining this balance was rooted in his understanding that not everyone approached ethics as he did. In other words, what good did it do to call racism a sin against the Christian God if many of the people he was trying to persuade didn't believe that racism was a sin or didn't accept the idea of God? Therefore, especially when speaking to audiences outside the church, King broadened his message by describing racism as an evil against humanity that destroyed the fabric of civilization. By describing the issue using terms that more people could relate to, King made his message more powerful without compromising his own beliefs. Instead of thumping his Bible, he thumped revered political documents such as the Declaration of Independence, the United States Constitution, and the Gettysburg Address. Even though King personally treasured his Bible more than these documents, he understood their value in making the case against racism to the American people.

Another of King's strategies was to use his ethical vision to focus on those issues that were most vital to attaining the greatest good for the greatest number of people. In order to accomplish this goal, King had to become tolerant of personal practices to which he otherwise might have objected. Also, because he wrestled with his own faults, he accepted others even when they failed to live up to his ideals. While not ignoring other social problems, such as alcoholism or teenage pregnancy, Dr. King reserved his greatest energies for his attack on racism because he understood that it contributed to many other social ills. He understood that if racism could be eliminated or even curbed, it would have a beneficial effect on many other evils in society.

Dr. King's example continues to be a model today for how we can work with others whose ideas about ethics differ from our own. We must use reasoning that can be understood by others who don't share our viewpoints. We should be tolerant of the ideas and behaviors of others, so long as they do not infringe upon basic human rights, and we should form coalitions among people of diverse backgrounds to promote ideals that will benefit all humanity.

These goals should be pursued with a sense of humility and compassion for human failings, but this does not mean that you should abandon your own personal framework of ethics and conduct, nor that you should give up promoting your personal ideas on ethics. Others may benefit from your views, and you should give them the freedom to agree or disagree with you and not attempt to compel them to accept your ideas. To force beliefs on others robs them of their personal dignity and usually backfires against you. Even self-destructive behavior, such as drug abuse, cannot be changed unless the person truly wishes to change. Ideas and behavior that do not stem from genuine convictions are usually abandoned in the long run.

# The Effects of Culture and Ethnicity on Ethical Viewpoint Formation

Culture and ethnicity are important influences on ethical viewpoint formation. Obviously, people from various nations and regions of the world have differences in their beliefs based on cultural distinctions, but clashes over ethics don't exist simply among people from different countries. As our nation becomes more diverse, people are increasingly finding that their friends and neighbors come from different cultural and ethnic backgrounds.

The role of culture and ethnicity can be especially important because of profound differences in values among various groups. Many Americans have a "Pepsi generation" mentality: People want to be young and active forever. Conversely, many non-Western cultures esteem age and maturity over youth and vigor. Ideas about work can also vary from one group to another. A Wall Street executive values productivity and efficiency, whereas the owner of a small neighborhood market may see relationships with customers as equally important.

The following table is a sample of the variables that exist among different cultures and ethnic groups.

# Variables Among Different Cultures and Ethnic Groups

| Culture A | Culture B |
|---|---|
| Time is thought of in precise terms. | Time is more generally regarded. |
| The emphasis is on punctuality and time management. | Being "on time" is fluid, depending on the occasion and circumstances. |
| After a certain age, parents are, at best, there only to give advice and offer opinions. | Parents continue to play a central role in decisions made throughout a person's life. |
| The rights and desires of the individual supersede those of the family or community. | Group needs take precedence over those of the individual. |
| Higher education is not regarded as vital to personal and vocational growth. | Higher education is a primary cultural value. |
| It is in your best interest to obey people in positions of authority. | The "authorities" are typically against you and should be resisted. |

As this table demonstrates, distinctions in cultural/ethnic values can make a major difference in a person's approach to ethics. Based on cultural differences, disobedience to parents may not be such a big deal for one person, yet to another it may be unthinkable. Study groups seem natural to people from cultures that encourage collaboration and cooperation, but students from cultures that reward individualism often prefer to go it alone, even though this approach takes more work. Sometimes working with others seems like cheating for these individuals.

## Moral Decision Making

Developing your own ethical viewpoints and understanding the viewpoints of others who differ from you is only one piece of the ethics pie. How you act within your own ethical framework is just as important.

By consistently acting on your own principles, you develop a sense of personal integrity. When you violate your own standards of conduct, you fracture ideals that are important to you and others. Obviously, no one is perfectly consistent in applying their values to life. Sometimes you need to forgive yourself and ask others to do the same. But it is important to make a good-faith effort. If you find that you cannot do what you believe in, perhaps you should reevaluate your beliefs or make some basic lifestyle changes. Often counseling professionals or religious leaders can assist you with this process.

Another dimension to moral decision making is ethical dilemmas. Most of the time, it's obvious what you should do (even if you don't want to do it); at other times the best choice is not so clear. Whenever two or more ethical values conflict, you may need to choose the greater good or the lesser evil. This point can be demonstrated with a brief look at a biblical tale.

### Lying and the Hebrew Midwives

The Bible is known for its moral teachings, which include telling the truth. In one story, however, the Bible says that God blessed people who lied. The story is in Exodus 1:15–21 and is about two Hebrew midwives who lied to Pharaoh. Although Pharaoh had commanded the midwives to kill any newborn Hebrew boys, they let the babies live because they knew it would be wrong to commit murder. When Pharaoh asked them why they did this, however, they did not give him the real reason. They lied by telling him that they were unable to kill the boys because the Hebrew women were vigorous and gave birth before the midwives arrived. The story goes on to say, "So God was kind to the midwives … and because the midwives feared God, he gave them families of their own."

# Ethical Scenarios

The following scenarios will give you some practice in making tough ethical decisions on some issues. As you think through your responses to the questions, ask yourself what your answers say about your true ethical values as opposed to your professed ones.

1.  a.  You have found out that your best friend and several others stole a copy of an exam that is to be given next week and are memorizing the answers. The exam

promises to be very difficult, and the instructor uses a curve. Their collective scores could significantly raise the curve since the class is not very large. What would you do? Remember that to do nothing is to do something.

b. Now imagine the same scenario, except that one of the other people in the class is a returning adult student whom you have gotten to know. She is having a terrible time with the class, and she needs to do well on the exam to get into her major. She was recently divorced and is attempting to support her two children while she attends school. You don't know her well, but you respect her greatly because of her determination to put her life together again. The cheating could raise the curve so much that it could hurt her chances to do well in the class. The thieves will not share the exam for fear of being discovered, and you are sure that she would not cheat anyway. Now what would you do? If these circumstances made a difference to you, why?

c. Imagine the same scenario again, except that now the one to be hurt by the curve is the person to whom you are engaged to be married. He or she is a good student who has expressed disgust over cheating because it makes the curve tougher; your partner is doing okay in the class, but really needs to get an A to get into medical school. You know that if your partner finds out, he or she will immediately go to the instructor. Now what would you do and why? If you answered differently here than in parts a and b, what does this tell you about your system of ethics? Identify some problems with the viewpoint "Just look out for number one."

2. Both of your roommates are very political and are divided over a number of issues, including affirmative action. As might be expected, the one who is opposed is white, and the roommate who is for it is African American. One evening their argument turns ugly and they almost come to blows. You decide to try to intervene in a positive way. What would you tell them?

A quick look could give you the answers you need. Should you? Could you?

3.  Your brother has been diagnosed with a life-threatening disease. His physicians have said he will die in six months. The only treatment is an experimental drug that has not received FDA approval. Although it promises to be very effective, it cannot be obtained unless the patient is part of a pilot study group. He applied to be in this group but was turned down because of space limitations. You work in the hospital that is doing the study. You know that you could steal enough of the drug to give your brother a course of treatment and not be caught. But because supplies of the drug are limited, this would mean someone else would not get treatment and would die. Furthermore, by stealing the drug, you would disrupt the study and cause a delay in the drug's release, which would cause hundreds of people to forgo treatment and die. What would you do and how would you justify it?

# Conclusion

Ethical viewpoint formation is an ongoing process that lasts your entire lifetime. Going to college will probably have a significant impact on your views, and it is important to think through how its impact will affect your beliefs. Acting on your beliefs is equally important to maintaining a consistent ethical approach to life. It's easy to avoid the issues or to simply watch your own back, but these approaches create an ethical vacuum that can ultimately work against everyone. The best ethical framework is one that leads to a sense of personal integrity and community responsibility. Moreover, it's just as important to respect the values of others who come to different good-faith conclusions.

Ethical conflicts can be especially sharp when disagreements arise from cultural or ethnic diversity. To be understanding and tolerant of the convictions of others, it is not necessary to take the position that there is no absolute right or wrong. People should contribute their ideas in ways that allow them to recognize the viewpoints of others without compromising their own belief structure. People who maintain this sense of balance are most satisfied with themselves and their relationships with others. An open attitude toward those who are most different from you can provide the best opportunities for growth and learning.

# Resources

Goodpaster, K. E. and K. M. Sayre, eds. *Ethics and Problems of the 21st Century*. Notre Dame, Ind.: University of Notre Dame Press, 1979.

Anscombe, G. E. M., *Ethics, Religion, and Politics*. Oxford: Blackwell, 1981.

# Chapter 7

# College and Women of Color

### Shawn Arango and Marc Levey

**W**omen of color have special challenges when it comes to attending a predominantly white institution (PWI). Not only are we faced with the usual challenges met by every entering college student—adjusting to a new environment, making new friends, choosing a major, the freshman fifteen—but we must also deal with the impact of being both a person of color and a female person of color. Although many books have been written about women in college or about being a student of color in college, few have attempted to merge these two traits and evaluate successful navigation techniques for women of color.

## Special Challenges for Women of Color at PWIs

As a woman of color, your experiences will vary from those of others, of course, and will even be contextual, but there is one common thread throughout your experience: You are a Black, Latina, Asian, or Native American woman, and this will affect the way you interact with people and how they interact with you.

When we see and interact with other people, we notice virtually everything about them physically, and our interactions are based on our *perceptions* of what we see. Denying that we notice a person's race or ethnicity is like claiming not to notice a pregnant woman's large, protruding stomach—it is not very likely. If you didn't notice that the woman was pregnant, you would be less likely to be sensitive to signs of her pregnancy, such as fatigue and all the other conditions that accompany the condition. The point here is that it is also important to notice uniqueness in each individual, because it can help enhance and direct our interactions.

But how do you know that the combination of your race and gender really matters to your success in college? To address this issue, let's look at how both race and gender play out in a variety of settings.

### In the Classroom

In the classroom you will have to deal with issues very similar to those encountered by white women: The professor who thinks women are not as quick as men. The instructor who tells sexist jokes, the frustration of being picked last for engineering lab, the classmate who leers at you.... The list goes on and on.

The special challenge you face will be to deal with all that *and* the added issue of being a person of color. This may add the new dimension of racism or prejudice. Skewed thinking can change a professor from one who thinks all women are a bit slow to one who thinks this is especially so for Black or Hispanic women. It can change the instructor who is sexist to the instructor who is sexist *and* believes the stereotype that Black and Hispanic women have stronger sex drives than other women. Maybe you will get lucky. You may meet a professor who believes that men and women are equal—*white* men and women, that is. The odds are not in your favor that every professor you have will be aware of the issues and pressures facing women of color.

This does not mean that professors will openly display racism or sexism. It simply means that you may feel extra pressure as a woman of color, especially as a first-year student, where you could find yourself in a class of five hundred and be the only woman of color.

You may also find yourself in an interactive class dealing with social issues, where the instructor might take up race or gender issues and solicit your opinion on the topic. All of this usually starts innocently enough, but what might be happening is that you are asked to speak for your entire race or sex, when quite frankly you are not an expert. None of us is. Like anyone else, we can simply speak in generalities based on our experiences in our families or neighborhoods. Speaking out is okay, because there is always the chance you will enlighten someone. Just make sure that the class knows you are speaking mainly for yourself and that what you say should not be construed as the viewpoint of your race or gender.

Sooner or later you will hear someone use the phrase "chilly classroom climate." This term has been used to describe the environment for women in many classrooms. According to research, women are called on less often, asked lower-order questions, may be addressed by their first name or called "hon" or some equally inappropriate term, and are too often treated as less competent than their male counterparts. This affects not only undergraduate students, but female graduate students as well.

Life is not always easy for women administrators and faculty members either, many of whom have to worry about the "glass ceiling," a term that refers to the invisible level above which no woman, regardless of skill, can expect to ascend. Female faculty members also face challenges in the classroom, with male students who may not believe they are competent, especially in certain disciplines in science, engineering, and medicine, traditionally held to be the bastions of males. Women professors sometimes must go to extraordinary lengths to prove the legitimacy of their research when the object of their study is feminism or race. Choosing these research topics may affect their chances for promotion or tenure.

If you think that you have been a victim of the "chilly classroom climate," talk to someone about it. If you feel it is bad enough, consider filing a complaint. I suggest you try the affirmative action office on your campus, the center for women students, or the Women's Studies Department.

## Student Life for Women of Color

At predominantly white institutions, you typically find students at the extremes of cultural awareness. Students of color who hail from the inner city are typically experienced with dealing with whites, and may even know how to interact successfully with whites in the classroom. What they may not be prepared for, though, is living with, eating with, and, quite frankly, being surrounded by whites. The typical minority enrollment at a PWI is not greater than 10 percent—and this estimate includes all American-born minorities and sometimes international students. Close your eyes and imagine yourself in a room with 100 people. Out of those 100, only 10 are people of color—maybe only 2 are Black and 2 are Hispanic. Imagine those same 100 people with you as you eat, sleep, party, study, and exercise.

For some of us, this spells real culture shock. In a situation like this, one of two things usually happens: (1) You totally immerse yourself in your culture, actively seek out people like yourself, and actively participate in events that celebrate your heritage; or (2) you keep going through your daily routine and adjust to "hanging" with whites. You begin to frequent white fraternities and basically try to ignore the issue of race. You even decide that a historically Black sorority does not meet your needs and decide instead to rush a white sorority.

This type of behavior typically occurs more with Black and Hispanic males than with females, and becomes a point of contention with many Black and Hispanic females when it comes to dating. On most predominantly white campuses, and in many communities for that matter, there is a shortage of available ethnic men. For a variety of reasons, there are precious few available men of color who choose to attend college or other post-secondary institutions.

It seems that numbers of Black and Hispanic men "discover" white women for the first time in college. White women are just as eager to explore new territory when they are not under the scrutinizing eyes of their parents. Some women are just plain curious about the sexual myths they have heard about. Others may be interested in dating

There is some pressure for minority women to date solely within their own race. This is not as true to the same degree for men, however.

the guy on campus who is considered to be "the man," for example, the star of one of the sports teams (or, in some cases, if he simply has a jacket meaning he made the team). Some men are interested in trying out these "Barbie dolls" who have been off-limits throughout their adolescence, yet presented to them through the media as the ideal of beauty and grace. It has also been my observation (and a joke among many of my male friends) that white women will put up with more and offer more financially to the men they are dating than will women of color. By this I mean that it is not uncommon to see Black or Hispanic guys driving the cars of upper-middle-class white women. Often these men are receiving cash, clothes, or groceries from these women, particularly when they are not in a financial position to do for themselves.

It is an infraction of NCAA rules for students on athletic scholarships to work during the season. This puts a cramp in the style of male athletes whose parents cannot afford to send them spending money. Some women also cook, clean, and do laundry for their new beaux. I know this may sound unreal, but believe me it will and does happen every day. And though such unbalanced relationships develop between same-race couples, they appear to be more common among relationships between Black and Hispanic males and white females.

Of course, there are a good number of interracial relationships that develop after high school that are based on mutual respect and healthy attraction, and these should be applauded and allowed to flourish. But many women are not interested in dating outside of their race. They are looking to date someone whom they would consider marrying, and to many, marrying outside of their race is a strict taboo or just illogical. Many women of color who attend college basically put their social lives on hold until they graduate. On the other hand, other women are able to enjoy very active social lives while in college, and some even meet their soul mates there. Without a doubt, however, women of color face special challenges when dating while attending a predominantly white institution, one of which is the way they are viewed by men.

## Male Views of Women of Color

The male view of women of color tends to vary with the social context and the racial/ethnic group of the observer. In general, white men subscribe to three schools of thought about women of color, and Black and Hispanic women in particular. The media has perpetuated the myth that Black women are self-reliant, strong, and, most important, domineering. This image has been carried forward in several television sitcoms, such as *Gimme a Break,* starring Nell Carter, and more recently in the person of Mrs. Winslow on *Family Matters.* This perception of Black women as aggressive is frightening to some white men. What is often overlooked is that this "aggression" is usually little more than what would be termed forcefulness in men, and is a result of the perseverance necessary for Black women to survive the struggles of their daily lives.

Another stereotype that Black and Hispanic women must endure on many campuses is that of the "hot mama." A good number of white men are physically attracted to women of color in an attempt to find an outlet for erotic passion. There is a common belief that Black and Hispanic women love sex and will be more sexually aggressive in bed than white women. Some white men might simply be curious; some might want to explore areas they would not dare to with what they feel are more reserved and less adventurous white women. An excellent example of this is the arrest of the actor Hugh Grant, who jeopardized his relationship with his model girlfriend to live out a brief fantasy with a Black hooker.

The third view you may encounter is that all Black and Hispanic women are from a lower socioeconomic class. People may assume that, because you are Black or Hispanic and a woman, you were admitted to college to fill a quota. They might also believe that you are less qualified than everyone else, are on financial aid, and live in the poorest section of an inner city.

Black and Hispanic men tend to view women within their cultures as domineering, usually recognizing that as a whole this group of women will not put up with a lot of game playing on the part of their mates. Some Black men choose not to date Black women during college for this reason, but will date Hispanic women.

Many men in college report that dating outside their race is acceptable, but bringing her home or marrying her is a different matter entirely. (*Dating*, in college men's terms, can range from having a serious girlfriend to seeing a particular woman only after dark.) Apparently, for some of these men, variety is okay in college, but serious relationships should still remain within the race. That is to say, Black and Hispanic men have respect for their women, but college is not the time they are mature enough to show it.

Of course, it is only right that we take a moment to give kudos to the Black and Hispanic men who enter college at a developmental stage where they are ready for a commitment. These men (few and far between) recognize women within their cultures as strong and worthy of respect, love, and admiration. You can usually find these men as active participants in student groups, as resident assistants, and in the library!

## Killing Us Softly: Media Stereotypes of Women

The aforementioned views of women of color are based in part on the media's portrayal of women in general, and women of color in particular. Female stereotypes are found in every aspect of life. Women's bodies are used to sell everything from cars to bug spray. The objectification of women has been an issue for many years. Not only does the media feed negative ideas about women to men, but the media also impact how women view themselves.

A prime example of this negative impact is body image. At some point in her life, almost every American woman will be on a diet. Many women are unhappy with their body images and strive to emulate the ideals of beauty thrown at us by the media: white skin, long blond hair, blue eyes, and a 38-26-36 figure. For many women the model look is not attainable—it simply does not match the body type with which they were born (and keep in mind that some models were not born with those bodies either). On college campuses across the country, anorexia and bulimia are so widespread that posters on the walls of dorm bathrooms warn of the dangers of self-induced vomiting.

The issue of body size seems to vary according to cultural preference. In many African American communities, men value women with "some meat on their bones"—that is to say, not obese, but certainly not model-thin. Genetically, it even seems that African American women are built with larger thighs and buttocks than their white counterparts.

The psychological burden of comparing oneself with a model image or striving for the perfect body is hard on women of all races. It can cause varying degrees of paranoia, insecurity, and obsession with food and exercise to the point where it becomes debilitating. Women of color are not only striving for the ideal body, they are also competing with not being of the "ideal race." So a Hispanic woman who considers herself nicely built may still have issues with her dark hair and eyes.

Some women also develop low self-esteem as a result of years of subliminal objectification. This leads to feeling that all the assets one possesses are physical and that they are all you have to offer a man. This disrespect also carries over to certain genres of music. Many rhythm and blues, pop, and rap songs describe women as having no other real value except for sex. Some songs frequently refer to women as "bitches" and "ho's." As a society we have become so desensitized to these terms that most people don't even flinch when they hear them being used in songs. We are raising a generation on this music, and our youth may develop their values from the street and pass this on.

As a college student, you should be aware of the media's devaluation of women and of your role as either a passive consumer or a fighter. Remember that there will be college men waiting for the first-year female students to arrive—what they consider "fresh meat." And be aware that any heightened awareness of sexism may cause you to be labeled a feminist.

## Feminism and Women of Color

The label of *feminist* can evoke very negative images in the minds of many men. It is often applied to a woman who is believed to hate all men. Obviously, this is not true, nor is it true that all feminists are lesbians. In essence, feminists simply recognize and protest the stereotypical and sexist representations and treatment of women in media and society.

Historically, the feminist movement has benefited white women more than women of color. In the minds of some scholars, too much time is spent by women of color on the subject of their exclusion from the feminist movement. Although this may be a valid point, it is difficult to separate your race and your sex. Who is to say which is more important? Each of us struggles with multiple identities, seeking to balance all the parts that make us whole. Women of color, although also striving for such things as equal pay for equal work, have had to struggle against several opponents simultaneously, many times fighting against racism and also fighting against the women who are supposed to be their allies.

Black feminism has its own unique challenges. Black feminists seek to recognize the strength of their great-grandmothers and strive to praise that strength while finding new and creative ways to pass on the legacy. Meanwhile, Black feminists are also combating the negative images and stereotypes of Blacks in general. Too many African American women have had a hard time trusting other women—Black or white—and this makes it difficult to build alliances.

A large percentage of Black women consciously try to maintain a more subdued role in the family in an effort to counteract the negative images of the Black matriarch and provide support and encouragement for their mates. Some women view their role as helping to restore the Black family in an effort to advance the race as a whole. Their place is at home, where they are most needed.

Unfortunately, Black feminists may often find themselves in a no-win situation. Challenged by the Black population, who can't seem to see past racism to the reality of sexism, much less the combination of both, Black feminists also struggle with finding their place in the movement. I encountered this dilemma personally in the classroom.

During a class I took as an undergraduate in college, I was involved in a group discussion with a woman who told me that white women had it just as hard as Black women during slavery. It was a tense moment for me as I struggled to control myself in that setting. Other group members turned their eyes toward me, and one friend finally said, "Well, what do you think about *that*?" He smiled because he knew I wasn't about to lose control. I proceeded to explain to the student that in my mind (and I consider myself a feminist) there was no comparison and no further discussion was needed. She stood her ground and insisted that we were in some way connected. Her theory was that during that period, white women were under the stern control of their husbands, needing to ask permission to do virtually anything out of the normal and beyond routine household tasks. Although we both considered ourselves feminists, we were rallying around very different issues. She was concerned with the right for women to drive and vote, whereas I was (and am) concerned with the inhumane treatment of women, largely based on their race. I am seeking to have people respect not only my gender, but also my culture and heritage, instead of considering me twice-stricken.

# Can I Make It? College Survival Strategies for Women of Color

Having been a two-time survivor of a predominantly white institution, I have compiled a number of strategies on how to increase your chances of success. These strategies are based on my personal experiences and observations and those of my friends, some of whom, unfortunately, did not make it through. Please do not view them as all-inclusive, but use them as a foundation upon which to build.

## Take Responsibility for Your Actions

As the old saying goes, You are the captain of your ship, the mistress of your destiny (or something like that). Basically, all this means is that even when the odds are not in your favor, you are still responsible for your own actions to the extent of at least trying your best to control your reaction to adversity. This philosophy should hold true as well in the parts of your life other than the classroom and your studies. This is especially critical when it comes to things like guns and drugs. Many people say that minorities do not put the drugs and guns in their neighborhoods and are therefore not responsible for all the drug use and violence. This may be true, but it is irrelevant. Why? Because *you* have control over whether you actually use those things or not.

There will be times during college when things seem so overwhelming that you cannot see anything working out. You have to convince yourself that it can be done and you are going to do it. You might have to be very creative. You may have to work an outside job or two. You may even have to eat oodles of noodles for a month (at five for a dollar, they are very popular on campus). If you are committed to completing your education, stick to it. The bottom line is to at least stay in control of yourself.

A good deal of the survival process in any post-secondary institution is a test of your perseverance. Keep the following things in mind when your school life seems too bleak to endure. First, most potential employers don't care that you have earned a hundred college credits if you don't have the degree. Also, many employers hire college graduates and then train them to perform specific job duties the company way. Your college degree tells the employer that you can be trained *and* that you have the discipline to stick with something you start and finish it. So do everything in your power to keep things rolling.

Here are some of the things you can do to take responsibility for your actions and ensure success:

- ✔ If you receive financial aid, make sure your financial aid applications are mailed on time and filled out completely and accurately.
- ✔ Make a conscious decision about whether to party or study—choose studying more often than partying.
- ✔ Choose to go to class rather than skip or sleep in.
- ✔ Get your assignments done on time.
- ✔ Be prepared to say no and to take the heat.
- ✔ Think of your future career all the time.
- ✔ Don't be too proud to seek tutorial help to enhance your grasp of the material.
- ✔ Do everything you can to keep your grade-point average (GPA) above a 2.50—this is the minimum that's necessary to give you a shot at a good job or the possibility of acceptance to a graduate school. In any event, a GPA of at least 2.00 is mandatory in most institutions to keep any federal financial aid for which you are entitled.
- ✔ Above all, be persistent.

One word of warning and encouragement: As you seek help, sometimes people don't have all the answers or they may give out misinformation, especially at large institutions where so many processes can become streamlined. If you're dissatisfied, keep asking questions until you feel you have exhausted all the options. If the answers you get are unacceptable, talk to the supervisors of people you spoke with. Get names of people who can give you information by phone. Let them know how important your education is to you. Above all else, don't lose your cool. Be polite, even in the face of disrespect or hostility.

## Learn How to Win Friends and Influence People

Some of you may know of the popular book by this title. Although I have never read it, I learned how important this principle was when I was in school. To me, it means knowing who your friends are and courting them actively. Navigating systems at any institution is challenging, but in a large "megaversity" it can sometimes seem impossible. The trick to getting more accurate answers is to change yourself in the mind of the faculty and staff from just another ID number to a living, breathing person. To do this, I recommend the following:

- ✔ Get to know one person in every office you deal with—registration, financial aid, advising—and always ask to speak to that person. Be sincere when you talk to people about your pressing issue. Learn their names and use them when you are talking to them.

- ✔ Whenever possible, conduct business early in the day and in person.

- ✔ Take a moment to ask whomever you are talking to about their day before plunging into information about you. Remember that they have families and feelings and they will have up days and down days. They will appreciate your concern for them and most likely will remember it.

## Find a Mentor

Finding a mentor should be very high on your priority list when you get on campus. People have varying definitions of what a mentor is and does, so for convenience let's define a mentor simply as someone who shows you the ropes. This could be an administrator, a faculty member, or an upper-class student. Some PWIs will try to provide a mentor for you, perhaps in the form of a buddy. I encourage you to participate in any such programs offered, but to take it one step further. If you don't click with your buddy, ask to be reassigned. If you still don't feel comfortable, begin the process of finding your own mentor.

Finding a mentor is not an easy task. Sometimes it happens when you don't even realize it; on other occasions it may seem like it will never happen. It seems to me that faculty and staff on campus singled me (and others) out as potential pupils. This was not something we discussed formally; it just kind of happened. As a matter of fact, a program at one PWI I attended set me up with a mentor and we never did get together. Instead, I spent time with other faculty and staff, finding out what they did and how they made it. Naturally, when I needed help, I went to them and asked their opinion. I have very fond memories of faculty giving me advice on topics ranging from my used car to parenting tips for my little one. I never forgot their kindness and still keep in touch to this day.

As you seek a mentor, be certain to check for a multicultural or minority affairs center or a cultural center on campus. This is always a good place to start looking for people who may be easy to talk to and concerned about your well-being. Also investigate any student groups that may represent your culture or ethnicity. Stop by—these are good places to meet down-to-earth folks.

## Use Academic Advising Centers

Many students of color enter college academically unprepared for the challenges to come. This is usually not by any fault of their own and can be remedied. Some colleges assign you an academic adviser who is trained to work with the needs of minority students. You should also be assigned an academic adviser through your academic college. Use them both. Use as many advisers as you can get. With proper academic advising, you can work toward graduation and move on to the next phase of your life.

## Develop a Strong Network of Friends

When I was an undergraduate, one of my mentors told me that most of my lifelong friendships would be made in college. At the time I was not sure he was right—after all, I still had my girls from high school, and we were still tight. But I later found that he could not have been more on target. All of my best friends now went to college with me. We formed a tight, small circle and always supported each other. That may not seem like much, but for us times were hard in college. Our friendship grew as we met challenges together and developed an extended family. If one of us had food, we all had food. We exchanged clothes, furniture, and rides. When I had an unplanned pregnancy during my junior year and decided to stay at college during the pregnancy, birth, and the early years of my daughter's life, my friends backed me up. Not only that, but they got up with my daughter in the middle of the night when I was overwhelmed. They made her bottles. They baby-sat until I could find permanent day care. They were there for me. To this day my daughter calls all my friends "Aunt," because that is how close they are to me—like sisters.

You may never encounter a situation as stressful as mine, but you will no doubt have your own crises. Make sure you select friends who will help you through; it can make a world of difference.

### Respect Yourself and Other Women

One of the oldest military tactics is to divide and conquer. This method is often used by men regarding women. Nevertheless, you must respect yourself enough not to engage in the catty behavior that men often associate with women. Remember that your primary reason for being in college is to obtain your degree, not win a mate. The energy you spend worrying about some girl who is chasing your man can be put to much better use. And the bottom line is that if he wants to go, nothing you can do will stop him.

Also, try to respect other women. It doesn't matter if they are white, Black, Latina, Asian, or green. They deserve a basic level of respect from one human to another. Try not to waste time engaging in name-calling and other negative behavior. Be bigger than the situation. You may not win the battle, but you will win the war.

### Delay Gratification

This is probably the toughest piece of advice to heed. Delaying gratification is especially hard when you go home to visit and your friends who started working right after high school are all driving new cars and wearing new clothes. You have to believe that what you are doing will help prepare you for a better life financially. Sometimes the job you get may not pay much better, but with your degree you may advance more quickly or secure a job with more flexibility. It may not seem very important to you now, but as you continue to mature, these quality-of-life issues will make the difference. Four years is a long time in one sense, but in the overall scheme of your life it is a very small investment for a major, lifelong return. Just hang in there!

## Conclusion

I hope what I have shared with you has been helpful. College is a wonderful experience—well worth the effort and the wait. For women of color, college at a predominantly white institution will have its challenges, but it has rewards too. Remember who you are and where you came from and I am sure you can make the most of your college experience.

# Chapter 8

# College and Asian American Women

Jung En Choi, Joe Schall, and Marc Levey

In her book of poetry, *The Phoenix Gone, the Terrace Empty*, Marilyn Chin describes her life as a first-generation Asian American woman; she defines the particular dilemmas faced by Asian American women as they struggle with their cultural and personal heritage, the expectations of their families, and the daily challenge of an existence that includes a "hyphenated identity." This chapter explores these same issues for Asian American women in college.

Describing any cultural group is difficult in that one must define characteristics of the group without cultivating stereotypes or trivializing the value of the individual. Describing Asian American women in college is especially difficult, because there are dozens of ethnicities within the Asian category, and each ethnic group is marked by distinct cultural and linguistic differences. Some Asian Americans have lived in the United States their entire lives, whereas others have immigrated only recently. Also, there is great variation in how much and in what ways a woman feels she is American or Asian.

We can begin by acknowledging that Asian American identity is too complicated to portray in one or even several profiles. There is no such thing as a "typical" Asian American. Furthermore, some women have thought a lot about what it means to be Asian American; for others racial identity has not been much of an issue. Some cannot speak their native language, or have been exposed to their native culture only through traditional customs still practiced in their homes.

Whatever the case, Asian American women typically deal with issues of cultural identity throughout high school and into college. This chapter uses interviews and research to identify these issues and draw conclusions about how Asian American women can cope with the challenges that college brings.

# Perceptions of Asian Americans: The "Model Minority" Stereotype

Perhaps it seems illogical that Asians, who are of vastly different ancestral backgrounds such as Chinese and Indian, are typically lumped together as one seemingly homogeneous group. Nevertheless, such a grouping underscores a fundamental problem faced by Asian Americans: As opposed to other minorities, Asian Americans are commonly perceived as "unassimilable foreigners"—outsiders who will never truly be assimilated into American culture. In her book *Unraveling the "Model Minority" Stereotype*, Stacey Lee (1996) demonstrates the political dimensions of this perception, noting how many universities, in defining minority scholarships and recruiting minority students, exclude Chinese, Japanese, and Korean Americans. In fact, Dana Tagaki's research (1992) on Asian Americans in higher education found that Asian American students are often perceived as being "at odds with university goals of diversity, in terms of either, and sometimes both, academic achievement and racial mix of the student body." Furthermore, the national census lumps all of the Asian nationalities together, and statistical data gathered from the census are used for researching demographic and enrollment trends, which determine certain policies in higher education for Asian Americans—for example, the focus of recruitment efforts and funding for special programs.

Such perceptions and political choices do far more than simply lump Asian Americans together as one group; they also underscore perhaps the greatest cultural challenge that Asian Americans face: being perceived as a "model minority." Due to slanted media coverage and the high-profile success of some Asian Americans, distinct stereotypes have developed about members of this group. The common stereotype is that Asian Americans are quiet, accepting, industrious, and financially successful. The belief is that, as students, all Asian Americans are mathematical whiz kids who will grow into hardworking, thrifty, efficient, and technically minded entrepreneurs. Asian Americans are "good minorities with correct social mobility," the stereotype goes; and when Asian Americans are even included in discussions of race, it is usually to talk about their "success" (Lee 1996).

# Perceptions of Asian American Women in College

Asian Americans face particular cultural challenges, and these challenges impact on Asian American women in college in numerous ways. Even though the experiences of Asian American women in college can differ greatly, college life for these women typically means balancing distinct sets of personal, cultural, and familial values, struggling with ethnic and racial identity, and making decisions about where allegiance lies when the different cultural values conflict. Because life in college is defined by flux, and racial identity is often fluid, an Asian American woman in college can expect a great deal of challenge and change.

Furthermore, an Asian American woman in college can expect to encounter the stereotypes that make such issues as racial identity, social life, and academics more complex. Stereotyped as academic superstars because they are Asian while facing the same struggles as other women in the professional world, Asian American women typically encounter varying responses from their peers, professors, and potential employers when it comes to their academic achievement. Struggling with such issues as identity development, racial bias, cultural stereotypes, academic expectations, and social life, Asian American women in college face challenges that are unique and ever present.

## Background of Women Interviewed for this Chapter

In developing the material for this chapter, the authors spoke with numerous Asian American undergraduate women about their transition from high school to college. These women were of various backgrounds: Chinese, Taiwanese, Korean, Vietnamese, Filipina, and Indian. Most of these women were born and raised in the United States; one woman moved to the United States with her mother while in her teens. Most of the women went to schools that were predominantly white. They were often the only Asian student in the class. Almost all described their socioeconomic status as middle class. In the interviews they discussed experiences with racism, ethnic identity, family life, academics, social life, and dating.

## Racism and Its Effect on Identity Development

In her essay "Growing Up Asian in America," Kesaya Noda (1989) reflects on the development of her ethnic identity: "A voice from my childhood says: 'You are other. You are less than. You are unalterably alien.'" People would address her with such curious comments as "You don't like cheese do you?... I know your people don't like cheese." Finally, Noda defines the dilemma of identity development for the Asian American woman by questioning, "How is one to know and define oneself? From the inside—within a context that is self-defined, from a grounding in community and a connection with culture and history that are comfortably accepted? Or from the outside—

in terms of messages received from the media and people who are often ignorant?"

Undeniably, racism plays a part in identity development for many Asian American women. Exactly how prevalent racism is toward Asian American women is difficult to assess. Whereas some Asian American women may not encounter it directly, others meet with racial slurs. They are laughed at for their physical features such as eye shape or facial characteristics, or mocked with exaggerated forms of so-called Asian accents. These comments often come from males, who simultaneously attack the woman's self-esteem and her heritage as a person of Asian descent.

Regarding racism prior to college, the Asian American college women interviewed reported a great range of experiences—from having been harassed throughout childhood and high school to virtually none at all. One woman said that most of her encounters occurred when she was young. She described being discriminated against for a long period by an elementary school teacher. Another woman who reported not having been harassed speculated that she didn't recognize the subtle racist incidents. She recounted an incident in which she and some other Asian women met with racial slurs and mocking on campus, but she was the only person of the group who didn't feel upset by it and did not retaliate with her friends. Similarly, one student denied that racism was an issue for her growing up, but also related that her brother was beaten up because he was Asian.

A Chinese sophomore reported that she and a female Korean friend were taunted with a "Go back to Korea" comment by a couple of white females on campus. She also said that the cashier at a local student supplies store ignored them or refused to bag their purchases. Another student reported perplexity at unusual behaviors directed toward her and her parents. She stated that she was mostly aware of racism by the way employers treated her father. Another student also encountered racist remarks from professors.

Finally, a Chinese student related that she had never encountered much racism in high school, but in college some men shouted Kung Fu jokes as she and some Asian friends passed by a dorm room. Later, as the friends discussed the incident during lunch, one of the men who had made the remarks overheard the discussion and approached them. He forbade them from ever calling him "racist," and then commented darkly, "There are so many of you."

What these accounts demonstrate is that, like other minorities, Asian American women may encounter outright racism in college. If they do, it is likely that the racism will be based on physical appearance and will complicate the woman's struggle to feel comfortable in a culture where issues of identity for college women are always complex.

## Academic Expectations of Asian American Women

Many parents of Asian American women encounter racism and feel culturally isolated—this is just one of the reasons why many parents believe it is important that their daughters attend college in order to increase the likelihood of securing a prestigious job. Especially for those parents and daughters who recently immigrated to the United States, there is often a great deal of concern about how women are perceived in their native culture, and academic decisions are made accordingly.

There is a strong stereotype that Asian parents put an enormous amount of academic pressure on their children. In the group of students interviewed, however, most reported that their parents ultimately did not view grades as a measure of true success. Furthermore, most of the women stated that their own measures of success were not based on grades, but on whether or not they were happy with their work and their decisions.

Another prevalent stereotype about Asians is that they are naturally good students who are especially gifted in math and science. Reviews of the statistics on Asian American academic performance at a state university, however, reveal that there are many students in this group who show average or below-average performance, as well as a significant number who do not perform well at all. Certainly, there are Asian American students who excel, but the percentages of these students seem too small to validate the generalization suggested by the stereotype.

Several interviewees reported that their parents were very concerned about money. One woman attributed this, at least in part, to her parent's cognizance of the class system in India, her native land. A Korean student reported that her mother was also especially concerned with money, and she wanted her children to be able to survive independently.

Despite parental concerns for their daughters' financial futures, the students interviewed reported that their parents did not pressure them to choose a specific major—they were encouraged to make their own decisions. This result runs counter to the widely held view that most Asian American parents are more dictatorial than white parents. As in every culture, there are different degrees of how much influence parents try to exert in career or major selection, but many parents see the wisdom of letting the student make the choice for herself.

Certainly, there are many Asian Americans who have enjoyed academic success. In fact, among minorities, Asian American students have the lowest high school drop-out rate in the nation (Hsia 1988). Evidence also suggests that Asian Americans are more likely than white students or other minority students to complete a college degree at the school where they began their studies (Hsia 1988).

We must still be careful with stereotypes about Asian Americans in college, however, especially because they can disregard individual experiences and development or direct students into fields where they perceive they should be because of cultural stereotypes. For instance, even though many Asian Americans choose engineering fields, higher-education literature cites a theory that this tendency can be attributed to a belief that there is less discrimination in technical fields, where success is not necessarily contingent on one's English-language skills. Several of the students interviewed had aspirations for careers in creative fields, such as theater or acting, but were discouraged by what they perceived as limited opportunities that were grounded in their ethnic identity. As stereotypes about Asian Americans grow, those women whose academic accomplishments and decisions run counter to what the stereotypes would suggest can feel especially alone and unsupported.

## Family Life and Social Life

Home life is important for many Asian American women, and many come from what may be described as a typical Asian household in America—that is, one that is father-dominated, with traditional etiquette that respects a patriarchal order. As a result, some Asian American parents can be restrictive, especially when it comes to their daughter's social life. In contrast, other parents of Asian American women, often greatly aware of the "dual ethnic identity" that their daughters live with, balance the familial tradition of a native culture with their daughter's needs as a young person living in a modern North American culture. For instance, as revealed in her study of Korean American students, Eun-Young Kim (1993) found that a majority of Korean students studied had taken "American names," reflecting their parents' desire to help them be accepted into American society.

For Asian American students whose families adhere to strict cultural rules, maintaining a satisfying social life can be especially difficult. A few of the students interviewed reported having to lie to their parents in order to maintain a social life, feigning work on a school project in order to get permission to stay over at a friend's house. In the most strictly run households, there was often tension between parents and their daughter when she visited home during semester breaks.

Most of the women interviewed, however, said that there was constant negotiation and flexibility when it came to social rules. For example, some women reported that their parents encouraged them to become integrated into American culture and wanted them to attain fluency in English, viewing this as a skill key to success in America. Because the students interviewed grew up in America, they for the most part felt they had more in common with mainstream American culture than with their traditional ethnic culture. They noted that most of their friends were white. A few of the women reported that they had a circle of intimate Asian friends, but still had friends of different backgrounds. Those women who reported feeling more comfortable with their Asian friends attributed this to the sharing of certain family dynamics that came from their traditional cultures.

Ultimately, the question of social life for Asian American women in college often becomes less a matter of family expectations and customs than it does ethnic identity. The fact that Asian American women in college frequently feel that they have to forge a dual identity has a great impact on their social lives. The tendency is to view certain friends as Asian friends and others as American friends, and it can be difficult to find a connection between these two groups. A few of the women interviewed even reported feeling especially uneasy with some of their Asian peers, who made them feel as though they weren't "Asian enough." These women sometimes felt like outsiders among both their American and Asian friends.

## Issues of Dating for Asian American Women

As with issues of social life, issues of dating for Asian American women are often strongly tied to the expectations of their parents and family, which can be restrictive. For most of the students interviewed,

Asian women report that they make friends outside their racial/ethnic group once they reach college.

high school dating was completely out of the question. These students said that their parents strongly disapproved of dating. They understood that not only were they not permitted to date in high school or college, when the time came they were expected to marry someone within their ethnic group. One of the Indian and two of the Korean women interviewed reported that their parents were still hopeful for an arranged marriage. One woman even reported that she hadn't rejected this as an option.

The greatest emotional challenge for Asian American women as they attempt to date in college can be dealing with the perceptions of their potential partners. As Renee Tajima notes in her essay "Lotus Blossoms Don't Bleed: Images of Asian Women" (1989), Asian American women, in particular because of depictions in film, are often narrowly viewed as passive figures whose role is to serve males. As Tajima describes it, "Asian women in American cinema are interchangeable in appearance and name… The dozens of populations of Asian and Pacific Island groups are lumped into one homogeneous mass of Mama Sans."

The Asian American women interviewed were especially concerned with the complications of dating, and in some cases worried about being perceived as unattractive because they did not "look

American." Although some of the women did not date or only dated other Asian Americans, most of the women interviewed said that they had dated white students, and one reported having dated a Black student. A few interviewees wondered if Americans would find them pretty enough, and some involved in interracial relationships felt especially vulnerable to the possibility of racist remarks or curious looks from strangers. In some cases, too, the students reported having to date secretly without their parents' knowledge.

What the issue of dating underscores in particular is that, in addition to the usual challenges that college-age women face in choosing social partners, Asian American women must weigh the factors of family, race, and their own personal ethnic identity in making dating decisions. As the women interviewed confirmed in their responses to questions, the dating issue is an especially complex and troubling one.

# Advice to Asian American Women in College

By way of conclusion, the authors offer the following advice, based on the research and interviews done for this chapter, to Asian American women in college.

- ✔ Consider the "model minority" stereotype in relation to your life as a college student. Remember that a fundamental danger of stereotypes on the individual level is that they can dictate behavior, promote injustice, and stifle identity. Understand that this stereotype exists and come to terms with it through some self-examination and study. Discuss the issue with your peers if appropriate.

- ✔ Define what your cultural identity means to you and recognize that it is always evolving. As suggested several times in this chapter, some Asian American women can feel culturally isolated, and Asian Americans in particular can be perceived as "unassimilable foreigners." Resist the impulse to give into such thinking, and find ways to balance both your Asian and American roots.

- ✔ Study the heritage of your native culture and determine where it connects or does not connect with your life. Both the richness and the singularity of Asian cultures warrant such study.

✔ Understand that you may encounter racism in college, either subtle or overt. Find positive ways to counter such racism, be they through challenging individuals who practice it or by quiet personal growth.

✔ Strive for academic success, but not because of the "Asian whiz kid" stereotypes, and not to the point that you sacrifice your personal desires and motivations. Consider the wide variety of majors and career paths available, and resist notions that would limit or pigeonhole you unreasonably based on the fact that you are an Asian American woman.

✔ Seek a relationship with your parents that will support their traditions of cultural heritage but also accommodate your needs as a woman in college. As an Asian American woman, you have an individual heritage that will remain with you beyond college, and do not be too quick to reject your parent's wishes simply because of the freedom that college brings.

✔ In matters of dating, consider discussing concerns of cultural identity with your partner, who may have to face the same or similar concerns in a relationship with you. Understand the narrow media portrayal of Asian American women and its influence on you or your partner. At the same time, remember that the issue of dating is complex for any woman in college, and one need not further complicate it unnecessarily.

✔ Read books and articles, such as those referenced in this chapter, devoted to the subject of Asian American women. From the poetry of Marilyn Chin in *The Phoenix Gone, the Terrace Empty* to essay collections such as *Making Waves: An Anthology of Writings by and About Asian American Women*, there is a wellspring of relevant material available in libraries and bookstores.

# References

Chin, Marilyn. *The Phoenix Gone, the Terrace Empty* (Minneapolis: Milkweed Editions, 1994).

Hsia, Jayjia. *Asian Americans in Higher Education and at Work* (Hillsdale, N.J.: Lawrence Erlbaum Associates, 1988).

Kim, Eun-Young. "Career Choice Among Second-Generation Korean Americans: Reflections of a Cultural Model of Success," in *Anthropology and Education Quarterly* 24 (3), 1993, 224–248.

Lee, Stacey J. *Unraveling the "Model Minority" Stereotype: Listening to Asian American Youth* (New York: Teachers College Press, 1996).

Noda, Kesaya E. "Growing Up Asian in America," in *Making Waves: An Anthology of Writings by and About Asian American Women* (Boston: Beacon Press, 1989), 243–251.

Tagaki, Dana Y. *The Retreat from Race: Asian American Admissions and Racial Politics* (New Brunswick: Rutgers University Press, 1992).

Tajima, Renee E. "Lotus Blossoms Don't Bleed: Images of Asian Women," in *Making Waves: An Anthology of Writings by and About Asian American Women* (Boston: Beacon Press, 1989), 308–317.

# Chapter 9

# Relationships
# in College

**Karen Feldbaum**

$\mathbf{A}$s you begin your college career, it may be easy to get caught up in all of the pressures of starting out fresh in a new school, with new people and new situations in a new city, state, or even country. In all of the excitement, it's tempting to focus on everything else but yourself. And you will find that it's easy to lose your identity in the crowd. This chapter will assist you in an exploration of yourself and your relationships with others. For many years you have developed connections with friends, family, teachers, and members of your community, but now you are about to enter a new environment, where you will meet new people and develop new relationships. Who are you? What do you value? Who are your friends? What is important to you in your friendships? Have you thought about establishing connections with faculty? What about your roommates? Are you going to get involved in a student organization? As you work through this chapter, you will begin to find answers to these important questions.

## Developing a Relationship with Yourself

The most meaningful relationship you will ever have is the one you develop with yourself. This may sound a bit basic, but it's true. Before you begin to think about who you are in relationship to someone else, you need to think about who you are all by yourself. We don't often take the time to really think about who we are and what we are all about. You are unique in this world. There is no one else exactly like you. In college you will find that you have a lot to learn about yourself and others around you. You will also learn that you have much to contribute to your new community. Others have a lot to learn by being with you.

A part of acknowledging who you are is acknowledging that you may be the only person of color in your classroom, on your residence-hall floor, on a sports team, or in a club or organization you choose to join. For many people of color, it is not a rare experience to be in the minority, but for others it will be a major adjustment. The same holds true for some of the individuals with whom you come in contact. There will be white people who have never met a person of color before, let alone lived with one. Many whites have never had the opportunity to even have conversations with someone who is not also white.

Intellectually, it may be easy to understand that some people may make incorrect assumptions about you or not treat you the way you would like to be treated. But the hard part of adjusting to people's treatment of you may be dealing with the feelings that come along with your responses. It is important to find people with whom you feel comfortable talking about both the difficulties and the exciting, positive interactions that you experience living in a multicultural society.

When looking for support, there are a few people who come quickly to mind: Your friends, roommates, professors, or the residence-hall staff may be people you can turn to. There also will be some offices and designated staff people on campus to whom you can turn. The thing to remember is that you are not alone.

# Knowing Yourself

Do you ever take time to think about the contributions you have made to the world? As an exercise in considering how you view yourself, take a moment to complete the following open-ended statements:

*One thing I like about myself is*

_____

*My proudest moment was when*

_____

*One achievement I'm really proud of is*

_____

*One thing that I will contribute to the college or university community is*

_____

As you begin to get to know yourself, it may be helpful to think about how you like to spend your time. Although what you enjoy doing may change over time, when you find yourself in a new environment, it is tempting to adapt to whatever everyone else seems to be doing. Sometimes the hardest thing is to give yourself permission to do what you really enjoy, even if it doesn't make you popular.

The exercise on the following page will help you think about the kinds of things you like to do. Of the activities listed, circle the ones that you enjoy.

Reading                             Watching movies

Watching TV                         Participating in sporting events

Dancing                             Shopping

Eating out                          Taking walks

Talking with friends                Spending time alone

Attending sporting events           Running

Listening to music                  Playing a musical instrument

Spending time with family

What are some activities that you enjoy that are not listed?

_____

Now consider these questions: Do you prefer to do things alone or in a group? Of the activities circled and the ones you added, which are your three favorites? List them below:

1. _____

2. _____

3. _____

In college it is easy to let time get away from you. At the end of some days you will wonder where all of the time went. Even though you must remain very busy with schoolwork, it is important to reserve some time in your schedule for doing some of the things that you really enjoy. It is also important that you don't give up the things you enjoy just to fit in or be popular. You are your own unique person. It's vital that you honor who you are.

## Developing Relationships with Others

One of the foundations of developing relationships with other people is developing an effective communication style. Communicating in an assertive way will allow you to express yourself honestly and directly. When you are assertive, you stand up for your rights in a way that doesn't violate the rights of others. The assertive person makes his or her own choices, is confident, and feels good about himself or herself.

*Assertive behavior* is based upon the belief that every person has certain basic interpersonal rights. Among the most important are:

✔ The right to be treated with respect
✔ The right to have and express personal feelings and opinions
✔ The right to be listened to and taken seriously
✔ The right to set your own priorities
✔ The right to make requests or ask for what you want, knowing that others have the right to refuse
✔ The right to make mistakes
✔ The right to say, "I don't understand"
✔ The right to say, "I don't know"
✔ The right to say, "No"

Aggressive behavior and non-assertive communication are two other styles of communication that are often confused with assertive behavior. To clarify, *aggressive behavior* involves expressing your feelings and ideas at the expense of others. When you stand up for your own rights while ignoring the rights of others, you risk being viewed as an aggressive person. Although people who are aggressive may get their point across, they do so in a way that is often offensive to the people with whom they are trying to communicate.

*Non-assertive communication* occurs when you do not express your own feelings or ideas. In many cases, this means that you allow others to ignore your rights or make choices for you, as if you had no role in the process. Initially, this style may seem less stressful, but in the long run you are less likely to get what you really need.

The following situations occur frequently on college campuses. For each scenario, mark the responses as assertive, non-assertive, or aggressive. If you're not sure, take a guess.

| **Assertive** | **Non-assertive** | **Aggressive** |
| --- | --- | --- |

1.  *You're out with a group of friends, and you're all deciding which movie to see. One person has just mentioned a movie you don't want to see. You say:*

    a. That's a lousy idea. Your taste for movies is really rotten.

| _____ | _____ | _____ |

| Assertive | Non-assertive | Aggressive |
|---|---|---|

b. I don't want to see that one. How about a movie at the Bijou Theater?

   _____        _____        _____

c. Well, I don't know much about that movie, but I guess if you want to we can see it.

   _____        _____        _____

2. *You believe that you have been going out too much lately and decide to stay in one Friday night to study. Your friend is trying hard to convince you to go out. You say:*

   a. I don't want to go out tonight. I need to study and I want to stay in. I might be interested in doing something with you tomorrow night.

   _____        _____        _____

   b. Well, okay. I was going to study and I didn't really want to go out, but I guess I can always study tomorrow.

   _____        _____        _____

   c. Are you crazy? You know I need to study. Why don't you leave me alone?

   _____        _____        _____

3. *You are returning an item of clothing to a department store. You found a small hole in it that you hadn't seen when you tried it on. The clerk tells you to keep the item, saying "No one will ever notice." You say:*

   a. Well, are you sure no one will notice it?

   _____        _____        _____

   b. Look, just give me the money back. I don't have time to argue with you.

   _____        _____        _____

   c. That may be so, but I'd still like to return it or exchange it. I do not want to keep this one.

   _____        _____        _____

Most people would agree that the correct responses to the above questions are as follows:

| | | |
|---|---|---|
| 1a  aggressive | 1b  assertive | 1c  non-assertive |
| 2a  assertive | 2b  non-assertive | 2c  aggressive |
| 3a  non-assertive | 3b  aggressive | 3c  assertive |

Which types of responses seem most comfortable to you? Do you tend to react more often in an assertive, aggressive, or non-assertive manner? It may be important to practice responding to situations in an assertive way. If your first reaction tends to be more non-assertive or aggressive, you may find more success with assertive communication.

# Responding to and Resolving Conflicts in Your Life

Regardless of your own communication style, you will sometimes find yourself in a conflict-of-needs situation with another person. Development of conflict management skills will strengthen your ability to communicate your needs not only at school but throughout your life. These skills will come into play with your roommates and the friends and co-workers you may see every day, as well as family members and teachers. Keep in mind that all of your interactions have the potential to result in conflict. But conflict in itself isn't necessarily a bad thing. What may be destructive, however, are the ways you choose to respond to the conflict. You may also find that as you work through a conflict you will be drawn closer to the individuals involved.

### Creative Conflict Resolution

Effective conflict resolution does not mean one person wins and the other person loses. Creative conflict resolution often results in a win-win situation, where everyone gets some part of what they want or believe they need.

Here's an example: Suppose Cindy and Tanya are roommates in Johnson Hall. Cindy enjoys studying in the room, whereas Tanya feels the room is a place to relax, have fun, and listen to music. Conflict arises one day when Tanya comes into the room with a few friends and turns on the TV while Cindy is studying. Tanya wants to set the rule that whoever wants to study should do so at the library. Cindy feels that watching TV with friends should always be done in the TV lounge down the hall. Once both students explain what they want, they are able to come up with a compromise. The resolution: Certain hours of the day are set aside for quiet study, and some other times are open to friends for visiting.

It may be helpful to view working through a conflict as simply solving a problem. The following are some of the basic steps many people use when faced with a conflict they'd like to resolve.

1. Define the problem—what really is the issue?
2. Identify what each person wants from the resolution.
3. Determine what all possible solutions may be.
4. Pick a solution that all parties can agree to try.
5. Set a future time to get together to evaluate the resolution.

Take a few moments to think about a conflict using the worksheet on the following page. If you are currently involved in a conflict with another person, you may want to ask him or her to go through the process with you. You may also examine a previous conflict using the worksheet.

### Some Things to Remember About Conflict Resolution

When responding to and resolving conflicts in your life, it is important to remember the following points:

✔ There may be a positive value in conflict.
✔ Stick to the issues at hand, and try not to personalize the conflict.
✔ Always make it your goal to find a win-win resolution.

## Developing Relationships with Your Peers

Peer pressure is a phenomenon not only of grade school and high school but also on college campuses. As a minority student at a predominantly white institution, you may feel a lot of pressure to fit in, especially if you attend a college or university where you don't know anyone else. Try to remember that you are not alone. Most new

# Conflict Resolution/Problem-Solving Worksheet

1.  Define the problem:

2.  List what each person involved in the problem wants from the resolution:

3.  List some possible ways to resolve the conflict:

4.  Evaluate each of the possible solutions:

5.  Select and agree upon a solution to try:

6.  Select a future time to get together to determine if the selected option has been successful:

students are going through the same thing. Most of them, too, have not been alone on campus before and have not lived in a residence hall. Also, like you, they have inherited thirty or more new housemates on their residence hall floor. Many times you will find yourself in a group of new students who, like yourself, are just trying to figure out what they are "supposed" to do. It may help to remind yourself that college is a time to figure out what's important to you, to identify and develop lasting values.

During your time in college, you will meet many different people. Just as in high school, some will become friends and others will not. If you are one of a few students of color at a predominantly white institution, friendships may take on even more importance. There may be some people who want you as a friend just because you belong to a particular race. This may be a white person who has never had a friend of a different race, or it may be a person who believes that you should automatically be friends because you seem to share a common ethnic or racial background. Friendships develop for many different reasons, but you should never feel forced into a friendship just because someone else thinks you should. These are situations when peer pressure can be the strongest. In deciding who your friends should be, it may be helpful to think about what is really important to you about friendships.

Here are some important points to remember about friendship:

- ✔ A friend is a present you give yourself.
- ✔ Friendships take time to develop.
- ✔ Friendship should never be built on peer pressure.
- ✔ Friendship is based on mutual respect.

Although you may already have many friends, you may find as you enter college that there are many new people you'd like to include in your life. It may be helpful to spend some time thinking about what friendship means and some of the characteristics you look for in people. Take a few minutes now to do the following exercise. You may want to find some of the friends you already have and do it together.

*What I look for in a friend:*
I think being a friend means:

_____

_____

_____

_____

_____

_____

_____

I am a good friend because:

_____

_____

_____

_____

_____

_____

_____

Next evaluate your friendships further. How important are the characteristics listed on the chart on the following page in your friendships?

## Characteristics of Friendships

| | Important | Somewhat Important | Not Important |
|---|:---:|:---:|:---:|
| Age | ☐ | ☐ | ☐ |
| Gender | ☐ | ☐ | ☐ |
| Race | ☐ | ☐ | ☐ |
| Religion | ☐ | ☐ | ☐ |
| Academic major | ☐ | ☐ | ☐ |
| Attitudes about drugs or alcohol | ☐ | ☐ | ☐ |
| Attitudes about politics | ☐ | ☐ | ☐ |
| Sexual orientation | ☐ | ☐ | ☐ |
| Family background | ☐ | ☐ | ☐ |
| Sharing the same friends | ☐ | ☐ | ☐ |
| Attitudes about trust | ☐ | ☐ | ☐ |
| Attitudes about communication | ☐ | ☐ | ☐ |
| Compatible activities | ☐ | ☐ | ☐ |

# Intimate Relationships

There will probably come a time while you are in college that you decide to develop an intimate relationship with someone, apparent by your desire to spend more time with this person and the exclusive emotional or sexual feelings you experience. Typically, family and friends will have a great interest in whom you choose to date in college. Being clear yourself about the decisions you make will make it easier to respond to the reactions of others. If you are a person of color on a predominantly white campus, you may find yourself contemplating dating people of another race or ethnic background. How important are race and ethnicity to you? Is it as important in a friend as in someone with whom you want to share a more intimate relationship? To develop and maintain a healthy intimate relationship, you must consider these questions carefully.

Here are some things to keep in mind when thinking about intimate relationships:

1.   It is not necessary to date someone just so you won't be alone. You can prosper through college with close friends, even though there may be times when it seems like everyone else has someone special. It's okay not to be like everyone else.

2.   Having an intimate relationship is *your* decision. Sometimes you may feel pressure to develop a more intimate relationship with someone in whom you may not be interested, or if you are interested, you may not be ready. It's okay to say no to someone who has expressed interest in you. It is always your decision.

3.   Don't lose sight of what's important to you. Often when people get involved in relationships, they forget about what's important to them. Although relationships require compromises, there will be some things you won't want to and should not negotiate. For example, you may find yourself interested in someone who believes that he or she should date many people at the same time rather than focus on one person. Do you agree with this value? If not, maybe this isn't the best person for you to get involved with. Refer back to the exercises on activities and friendships. Your responses to those exercises are significant when making a decision about dating.

4.   If you choose to date a person of a different race or ethnic background, keep in mind that race could become an issue. For instance, although you may be perfectly comfortable dating someone of a different race, other people of both your race and your partner's may be uncomfortable and have difficulty accepting your choice. It will be helpful for you to discuss these challenges with your partner.

# Relationships with Staff, Faculty, and Administrators

New students often believe that the most difficult people to talk with on campus are the faculty members. You may feel a bit overwhelmed at the prospect of talking with your professors. But there are many advantages to developing relationships with the faculty and staff at a college, university, or any other post-secondary school. It is important to think of your professors as people who can help you. Not only are they able to assist you with a specific course, but they may provide help in a variety of other situations. Faculty know other faculty, and the connection can help you. It is also useful that faculty know who you are and are aware that you care about your education.

Research shows that interaction with faculty is an important factor in a student's success. Students who interact frequently with faculty are in general more satisfied with their college experience than students who never established such relationships. As a student of color, you may want to seek out faculty members of color as role models and for support. Because the number of faculty of color may be small, however, it is important that you expand your search to include white faculty members who are known to be helpful.

Did you have a teacher in high school who was particularly helpful? How did you develop your relationship with that teacher? Although your college classes may be much larger than those in high school, you can still develop relationships with your professors. One of the differences, however, is that you may need to plan ahead. Typically, professors have office hours, times when they make themselves available to their students. Take advantage of this opportunity, even if you don't have a specific problem or question. In a university setting, you often must take the initiative if you want a teacher to know you. Unlike high school, where teachers made it a point to know you and may have followed and encouraged your progress, most college or university faculty members will get to know you only if you give them a reason.

Some smart ways to develop relationships with your professors include the following:

✔ Find out when their office hours are and stop by.

✔ Try to find specific questions in the lectures or textbook to ask about.

✔ Ask questions and participate in class.

✔ Attend presentations or lectures where your professors are speaking.

✔ Hand in assignments on time.

During your college experience, you may come into contact with faculty who don't seem to be as helpful. There may be times when you feel that assumptions are being made about your abilities based solely on your race, ethnicity, or gender. Besides being frustrating to you, these assumptions may become detrimental to your success in the classroom. If you ever find yourself in this predicament, it is important that you seek out people whom you know you can trust. If there are other people in the school who have been helpful before, or if there is a particular staff or faculty member you know well, ask for assistance and guidance.

In addition to your professors, there are a number of other staff people and administrators whom you may want to get to know. Did you meet with someone in the admissions office when you first came to the school? If so, you may want to stop by and let him or her know how you are doing. You may also have been assigned an adviser either before or after you arrived on campus. In addition to academic assistance, this person may be invaluable in helping you with other situations. If you have come into contact with staff in the housing or financial aid office, these may also be important contacts during your time as a student. What is most important is that you maintain contact with people who have helped you along the way. They will prove to be invaluable resources at times when you may need some support.

## Residence Hall Relationships

If you choose to attend a college or university that offers on-campus housing, don't be surprised that, as a freshman, you will probably be required to live on campus. Research on college students clearly shows that students who live in residence halls their first year are more likely to be successful academically in their college career. These students are also more likely to develop positive faculty and student relationships. If you have a choice of living on or off campus, academically speaking you may be more successful if you opt to live on campus.

## Being Away from Home

Although some students attend college in the same town where their family lives, most students travel away from home. If this is your situation, you may become homesick. *This is normal.* Although you may feel peer pressure to adapt quickly to being away from the people you love and who care about you, it is normal to have times when it feels hard and almost unbearable. It's okay to feel the way you do. What's important is that you find some ways to get through the rough times. Here are some tips for when the going gets tough:

- ✔ Get busy. Occupy yourself with some tasks that get your mind onto something besides missing home.
- ✔ Contact your family—write a letter or make a phone call.
- ✔ Get together with friends at school.
- ✔ Talk with a staff or faculty member who has been supportive in the past.

## Communicating with Your Roommate

If you choose to attend a primarily white institution, you can assume that your roommate will likely be white. You may or may not be used to sharing close space with another person on a day-to-day basis. Even if you have lived in close proximity with another person, it probably was not with someone you had never met before. Remember that all relationships take time. If you think about any of the other important people in your life, you will realize that those relationships did not form overnight.

All of our life experiences have an impact on who we are and why we think about things the way that we do. The hardest part about meeting someone new is putting aside your assumptions about them. This may especially hold true if your roommate is of a different race than you. Both of you will have assumptions formed from a combination of personal experiences and society's images. What is most important is that you acknowledge your perceptions and allow an opportunity for each of you to be honest about what you think and how you feel.

Be open to differences. What makes a good roommate may be things that you haven't thought of before. The fact that you and your roommate are a different age, come from a different town, or are a different race or religion may not be as critical as what time you go to

Be aware that you and your roommate will be in close proximity to one another. Be flexible!

sleep at night or how clean you like your room to be. Having a successful relationship with your roommate will not happen by itself. It will be, like any relationship, something you will need to work on.

Do not assume that you should click with your roommate immediately; good communication is not automatic. Effective communication takes time and effort. Right from the beginning, it is imperative to talk honestly about what is important to you. Communicating is more than just talking, however—it's listening too. It's really hearing what your roommate says and doing your best to understand what he or she means. Because all of our experiences are different, it is likely that we won't understand things in exactly the same way.

Here are some important things to remember when communicating with your roommate:

- ✔ Think about what you want to say before you say it.
- ✔ Speak only for yourself.
- ✔ Listen carefully to what your roommate is saying to you.
- ✔ Verify your understanding to be sure that you heard what was intended.

Although we tend to assume that roommates will get to know each other easily because they live together, it is a good idea to put some time aside early in the term to intentionally develop your relationship with your roommate. Grab a few meals together, do your laundry, or just sit on the bed and talk without the TV or radio on. Getting to know someone does not happen all at once, but will be a process that will continue as long as you are roommates.

## Shaping a Good Relationship with Your Roommate

To make it easier for you to get along with your roommate, consider the following series of questions and issues as you establish and develop your new relationship. Designate a time when you and your roommate can sit down and talk through some of the responses each of you has to these questions. Try to schedule a time when you won't be interrupted and one of you isn't in a hurry. You may also want to discuss some of the questions and issues formally with others, while you are eating a meal or walking to class. Whatever the case, answer the questions seriously and do your best to understand each other's responses.

*Some Issues to Discuss with Your Roommate*

*Daily issues:*
- ✔ What time do I like to go to sleep?
- ✔ What do I think about having guests or friends visit?
- ✔ What do I think about sharing things such as food or clothing?
- ✔ What is the best way for me to let you know that I am not happy with something?
- ✔ What is the best way for you to let me know the same thing?
- ✔ How do we want to handle telephone messages or other messages?
- ✔ Are there times when we will have quiet in the room to study?

*Family, cultural, and ethnic background:*
- ✔ What I would like to tell you about my family is…
- ✔ My cultural background includes…

✔ What it is like to live with someone who is a different race than I am…

✔ My best friend would describe me as…

✔ The way I characterize my neighborhood, my city or town, and the people who live there is…

✔ What I'll miss most about being away from home is…

✔ What I look forward to the most about being away from home is…

✔ I spent my time before coming to college doing…

✔ I decided to come to college because…

*Personal values, preferences, and characteristics:*

✔ How I feel about alcohol…

✔ How I feel about dating…

✔ How I feel about drugs…

✔ The kind of music, arts, or entertainment I enjoy are…

✔ What I'm like when I'm not happy about something…

✔ What I'm like when I'm under a lot of pressure…

Listen to your roommate's responses carefully. Try to be non-judgmental, remembering that there are likely to be areas where you don't agree. That is to be expected. The important thing is that you understand your differences and figure out a way to get along if you disagree. When you are accepting and tolerant of differences among people, they will be more at ease with you; and you will be contributing to understanding, not just in your relationship with your roommate, but in all of your relationships.

## Using a Roommate Contract

Especially if conflict develops, it is often helpful to develop a roommate contract. For this purpose, many schools provide students with a form they can fill out during the first few days of their arrival on campus. A sample roommate contract follows.

# ROOMMATE CONTRACT

Welcome to independence! You have arrived in the real world; no one will wake you for that 8:00 A.M. class, wash your clothes, or ask if your homework is done. Now is the time to meet your new roommate(s) and make your own house rules.

Living with someone you do not know will present a challenge. Accept the challenge and work with your roommate(s) to create an environment conducive to study, relaxation, privacy, sleep, friendship, and FUN!

The limitation of space alone requires consideration by each party, roommates, and suite mates. Communication is the key, and a little consideration goes a long way.

| *Cleanliness*<br>*(when and by whom)* | *Personal Property*<br>*(clothes, stereo, TV, etc.)* |
|---|---|
| Garbage: | To be shared or borrowed: |
| Sweeping: | Not to be shared: |
| Daily pick-up includes: | |

| *Food Items/Snacks* | *Study Time/Quiet Hours* |
|---|---|
| Do we share: | Noise level: |
| Where kept: | One studies/one watches<br>TV/listens to stereo: |

| *Guests/Visitation* | *Smoking* |
|---|---|
| When: | Okay or not in room: |
| How long: | |
| How often: | Okay or not by guests: |
| Unexpected guests: | |

| TV/Stereo | Dirty Clothes/Laundry |
|---|---|
| Early: | Anything done jointly: |
| Late: | |
| Noise level: | Share laundry products: |
| Do we share: | |

| Communication | Costs |
|---|---|
| Telephone messages: | Shared food: |
| Mail: | Phone calls: |
| Other messages left by friends: | Cleaning products: |

When we disagree or are in conflict:

We, the residents of _____ (room number), have discussed and agreed upon these conditions. We may renegotiate this agreement at any time during the year.

Signed _____ & _____

Dated _____ & _____

*Remember, the Residence Life staff is here to assist you if there are problems you need to resolve.*

*Contact your Resident Assistant (RA) or Coordinator for help.*

*Good luck to you and your roommates!*

## Relationships with the Residence Hall Staff

Key to your success in college is building relationships with people who can be your allies throughout your college experience and beyond. Allies may be found in surprising places. If you are living in the residence halls, where most first-year students live, there will be many opportunities for you to develop relationships. On your residence hall floor, you will probably have a fellow student, usually another undergraduate, called a resident assistant or resident adviser (RA). This person is trained to assist you in many ways and make your stay in the residence halls a positive one. In addition to being knowledgeable about institutional policies and guidelines, residence life staff should also be aware of campus resources and student organizations that you may want to explore.

Probably the most important thing to know about the resident assistant is that he or she is there for you. If you have a roommate problem or difficulty with a professor, your RA should be able to help you directly or point you in the right direction. In most cases, the RA will also have a supervisor who has an office located in the residence halls. This professional staff member is also available to assist you with problems, from housing questions to policies on makeup exams.

Although you may find that most residence life staff are not people of color, they are committed to creating positive environments for all students in the residence halls. As a resident of the community, you have a right to a living environment that feels supportive. If you find that this is not the case, it is important that you let the appropriate people know so a change can be made. If your RA is not responding to you or others on your floor in a helpful way, you first need to let him or her know. Sometimes an RA may not be aware of the impact of his or her behavior. If you try this approach and are not successful, you should approach his or her supervisor. In either case, it is important that you clearly identify your concerns so that you can feel more comfortable in your environment.

## On-Campus Relationships

Your first year may seem pretty hectic with all your time spent studying, eating, and sleeping, but you should still find some time to get out and do something different, something that may help you effectively spond to the stresses of college life. Research shows that stud who are active in the university community will be more successful in their college careers than students who choose not to get involved. By becoming an active participant in your college experience, you will develop many of the relationships that will provide the support you need when times are more difficult. Although this may surprise you, success in your college experience depends on more than just grades.

Were you in student government or other leadership organizations in high school? If so, you will find a variety of opportunities in a university setting to utilize what you have learned. You can start where you live: Most residence halls have some type of student governing board, as do most student organizations. Intramural sports offer another way to get involved. If sports or student government aren't your interests, keep looking, because you're bound to find some other organization that will help you get involved and meet people you otherwise would not have met.

Many colleges and universities have fraternities and sororities. In addition to the more traditional Greek organizations, there are a number of historically Black fraternities and sororities, as well as newly emerging Asian American and Hispanic ones. You will find a variety of other organizations on campus that embrace goals you believe in or sponsor activities you enjoy. And if you don't find what you're looking for, why not start a new club yourself?

Another way to get involved and find support is through some of the religious organizations and programs. There will probably be a wider variety of religious organizations than you expected. With time you'll probably be able to find a place that feels right for you. Watch the university newspaper for days and times of services. You may also find social and educational programs offered by clubs with religious affiliations.

To give you an idea of the vast opportunities for involvement, here is a small sample of some of the types of groups often found on college campuses:

| | |
|---|---|
| Amnesty International | Latino Caucus |
| Black Caucus | Martial Arts Group |
| Eco-Action | NAACP |
| Horticulture Club | Red Cross |
| Science Fiction Society | Student Film Organization |
| International Christian Fellowship | Women's Concerns |

## Off-Campus Relationships

Some colleges and universities do not provide the option for students to live on campus. If this is the case, or if you choose to, you will find yourself looking for a living situation off campus. Many campuses have an office or designated staff person to help students find off-campus housing. There is often a list of available housing options as well as names of other students who are looking for roommates. There may also be bulletin boards with lists, or organizations that keep their own files of people with apartments to rent. If there are organizations you think you might join, check with their members for possible housing options. This may increase your chances of living with someone with whom you have things in common.

Unlike in a residence hall, you might need to find your own roommate or roommates. If possible, meet with your potential roommate(s) before signing a lease. When searching for people to live with, keep in mind the questions discussed earlier in the section on roommates. You should also prominently discuss issues about financial responsibilities (e.g., rent, telephone, electric and heating bills) before agreeing to share an apartment. Location may be another important consideration. You will have to account for commute time to campus. Walking, taking public transportation, or finding a place to park your car may all be issues to consider. (For a more in-depth discussion of off-campus housing, see chapter 2.)

## Developing Relationships in the Community

The campus and surrounding area are your community, especially when you live off campus. Although you may spend much of your time on campus, be sure to venture off sometimes to explore the town or city. A starting point in the community may be a local church. Oftentimes in college communities, the local churches provide programs to encourage college students to get involved and meet other church members. Take advantage of these opportunities.

Community members can also help you get the lay of the land, especially if you have the opportunity to talk with people who have lived in the community for a while. They can provide tips on everything from good restaurants and stores to the best place to get your hair cut. If you play your cards right, you may even find local families who "adopt" you and offer you a place to go for an occasion home-cooked meal.

You may also want to look into the political activities of the community. Often towns and cities hold open meetings, where you can find out who makes the decisions and why they make the decisions that they do. As a freshman you may not be that interested in community politics, but as you spend more time in a place or if you feel you've met with discriminatory practices, it may become more important how and what decisions are made. For example, what are the attitudes in the community about multiculturalism? Is there a fair-housing ordinance that is inclusive? Is there an awareness in the community of people of color?

There will also be a number of opportunities for you to volunteer at a local agency or nonprofit organization. Have you ever thought about being a Big Brother or Big Sister? Or working for the Red Cross or a local homeless shelter? More and more college students are spending their time volunteering in the community. Consequently, many universities have an office that helps place students with a program that needs them. If volunteering is of interest to you, check it out. You may also find a way to get academic credits for your efforts.

## Conclusion

Sometimes the thought of going to college feels overwhelming. You will be faced with new people, places, challenges, and opportunities. This chapter help you begin to think about yourself and the many new relationships you will be developing. The practices explored here are not just for the freshman year, but will be important resources throughout your college career. I encourage you to come back to this chapter often to refresh your interpersonal skills. Don't be surprised if some of your responses change. Change is part of the process of becoming who you truly are. Let your college experience be one that celebrates your individuality.

## References

Allen, W. R., Epps, E. G., and Haniff, N. Z. *College In Black and White, African American Students in Predominantly White and in*

*Historically Black Public Universities.* Albany, State University of New York, 1991.

Nettles, M. and Thoeny, A. R. *Toward Black Undergraduate Student Equality in American Higher Education.* Westport: Greenwood Press, 1988.

Ponds, A. W., "Black Students' Needs on Predominantly White Campuses." In D. J. Write (ed.) *Responding to the Needs of Today's Minority Students.* San Francisco, Jossey-Bass, 1987.

Sellers, J., Sagaria, M., and Peterman, D. *The Roommate Starter Kit* State College: RSK, 1993.

Upcraft, M. L. "Residence Halls and Student Activities." In L. Noel, R. Levitz, and D. Saluri, (eds.) *Increasing Student Retention.* San Francisco: Jossey-Bass, 1985.

# Chapter 10

# Lesbian, Gay, and Bisexual Students of Color

**Michael Mobley with Marc Levey**

**W**hen I attended Pennsylvania State University as an undergraduate, I was really excited about meeting new friends, learning from professors, and enjoying campus life. But, as an African American student on a predominantly white campus, I began to wonder if these goals were possible. There were fewer than nine hundred African American students on a campus with more than thirty thousand students. But it was not my race that I thought might be the big issue; it was my sexual orientation.

Before going to Penn State, I knew I was gay, yet this aspect of my identity was hidden from everyone else. I reasoned that no one would find out unless I told them or went to some meeting where lesbian and gay people gathered. In my very first semester, I felt alone and afraid. I would not deny being attracted to men, but I worried that if others knew, I would lose my roommate, African American friends, and heterosexual friends. And, most of all, I feared that no one would respect me. Somewhat to my surprise, when I did come out the entire world did not leave me. I was no longer lonely, because I met lesbian and gay friends. This support was great! And, most important, my African American and white heterosexual *true* friends did not leave me.

In relating this brief account of my coming out during college, I hope you will understand one major thing: I wanted to be accepted and respected by all my heterosexual friends—those in the African American community and the white community. If you are a heterosexual student, you may discover that a close friend is lesbian, gay, or bisexual. Will you be able to accept and respect this friend after learning of his or her sexual orientation? I hope that you will. This chapter offers information about the experiences of lesbian, gay, and bisexual students of color. I hope this information will help you be supportive of your friends in the same way that my friends were of me.

Beyond my personal experience, this chapter focuses mainly on the actual life experiences of African American, Asian American, and Latin American lesbian, gay, and bisexual students attending predominantly white colleges and universities. One of the specific challenges for these individuals is to be accepted and respected by members of their racial or ethnic groups as well as by members of the lesbian, gay, and bisexual community.

For students of color who are gay (for convenience, the term *gay* is used to refer to lesbian, gay, and bisexual students from here on, even though there is some controversy about its use as a generic term), this chapter focuses on important issues that might arise during college. It is my hope that gay students of color receive helpful information to assist them in developing satisfactory and successful interpersonal relationships with white student peers and faculty; with the majority white lesbian, gay, and bisexual student community; as well as with the racial/ethnic cultural community on campus.

Hopefully, for heterosexual readers, this chapter will provide specific information about the unique experiences of gay students of color and perhaps even help you to understand more about yourself, your own sexuality, and how to interact with these students.

# Voices: African American Lesbians, Gay Men, and Bisexuals

What follows are some quotations that demonstrate how some people of color feel about their sexual orientation:

*"My blackness is what you see first. I can cover up my being gay."*
—Anonymous (Johnson 1981)

*"Being Black and being homosexual, one forms a double consciousness of being oppressed. By forming a consciousness of being Black, I gradually came to form a consciousness of what it is to be gay and oppressed too."*
—Lionel Cuffie, founder of Rutgers Student Homophile League

*"Some of us [women of color] end up dropping out of planning groups or raising hell. We might want to work on the racism that's going on there, but racial issues are tough and people don't really want to talk about them."*
—Diane (Loiacano 1989)

*"And that is a real fear that I have ... I fear losing sanity, and so maybe that is the reason why I scrutinize people with such care. Because I do depend upon others' perceptions of me for validation, and I have been hurt so much by that in the past ... Because, I mean, living in an environment ... where there's been so many things that have told me I was freaky, I was crazy, I was stupid ... And how much I had to fight against that, and struggle ... I had just kind of forgotten how much I fought to remain sane. I lived in a world which wanted to tell me that I wasn't. And that was a real battle."*
—Larry (Loiacano 1989)

*"I had a white lover for three years of college, and we were doing fine until I started taking some course in African American studies. She couldn't understand what more I needed to know since I was already Black."*
—Anonymous (Wall and Washington 1991)

*"I probably can avoid gay detection. It's obvious that I'm Black. Being Black is the bottom line. People know that about me from hearing me talk or seeing me. I'm Black even when I'm not sexual."*

—Anonymous (Johnson 1981)

*"My family certainly knows I'm lesbian, but we would never talk about it. Since junior high school, I can remember being called a dyke, and I knew I was; but I didn't want anyone else to know, so I never said anything. I know that my mother knew because she never asked me about boyfriends like she did with my sisters."*

—Anonymous (Wall and Washington 1991)

*"The gay community is one I move through as a consumer/spectator/cruiser. It represents safety to be 'gay' but it does not validate women, non-whites, older people … I qualify my gay identity politically."*

—Anonymous (Johnson 1981)

These quotes reflect only a portion of the experiences of African American lesbian, gay, and bisexual individuals. My hope in sharing these voices is that you will hear firsthand expressions about how African American lesbian, gay, and bisexual individuals navigate during their life journey. As you read this chapter, you will be presented with more voices, from Asian American lesbian, gay, and bisexual individuals and then finally with voices from Latin American lesbians, gays, and bisexuals.

# Being a Gay Student of Color at a PWI

Many minorities find it challenging to fully be themselves on majority campuses. But being African American, Asian American, or Latin American *and* a lesbian, gay, or bisexual on a predominantly white campus (PWI) is an especially unique experience. You must constantly deal with issues about both race and sexual orientation. You are often forced to decide whether you will share your sexual orientation with others during college. Even if you do decide to be open about it, you may choose not to be open at work when you leave college. The expression of your sexual orientation may change over time, from one setting to another.

It's important to recognize that as a unique subgroup of the student population, African American, Asian American, and Latin American lesbian, gay, and bisexual students share similar experiences with other student subgroups. But there are obviously key differences among gay students of color, white gay students, and non-white and white heterosexual students. Also, it would be a mistake to assume that all gay students of color share a common world view or even have had common life experiences. As with so many issues of race and sexual orientation, there is an inclination among many individuals to apply stereotypes to entire groups. Interestingly, where there is, as I shall call it, an *intersection of commonalties,* it usually focuses on gender, race, or sexual orientation. For most people, any *intersection of differences* also focuses on gender, race, or sexual orientation.

It's important here to understand that we create dichotomies of the shared human characteristics defined as gender, race, and sexual orientation. So it is useful to begin by discussing the commonalties and differences in human sexual identity. Sexual identity is a common link among all students, whether they are gay, heterosexual, white, African American, Asian American, or Latin American.

## Sexual Identity: How Do I Know Who I Am?

Janice Rench (1990) writes that "understanding and accepting people who act or think differently or look different from us is essential for a more tolerant and nonviolent society. Understanding the many aspects of human behavior can be a confusing task, particularly when information is withheld. This is especially true when we talk about sexuality." When Rench talks about "when information is withheld," she is referring to how societal messages from our churches, schools, parents, and medical community often fail to openly acknowledge sexuality.

When was the first time you learned about your sexual orientation? Most of us formally learned some things about sexuality in health education class during adolescence. Often, we heard giggles and laughter as the teacher discussed different aspects of male and female sexuality. As adolescents some of us were attentive and curious about it; others were extremely nervous and uncomfortable. And some of us played it cool and calm, giving the impression that we knew all there was to know about sex.

Although male and female sexuality were probably explored in some detail, your teachers almost always focused on heterosexual intimate relationships. Rarely if ever were same-sex intimate relationships discussed; gay sexuality and intimacy were especially taboo. But if the teacher did discuss same-sex sexuality, it was probably another time when you heard those nervous giggles. We also heard classmates making jokes, derogatory remarks and comments, and targeted teasing about lesbian, gay, and bisexual people.

It is important that you now, as college students, reflect on your own personal understanding of sexuality. As a young adult, possibly being away from home for the first time, you are in complete control of how you express your sexual identity and with whom you express it.

## Three Components of Sexual Identity

From the work of social scientists (Money, 1986; Hoyenga & Hoyenga, 1993) three components of sexual identity are constructed: (1) gender identity, (2) sex role behavior, and (3) sexual orientation.

It is important to understand how these three components work together to compose one's sexual identity. Understanding one's gender, sex role behavior, and sexual orientation can sometimes be difficult and confusing. Not all men are masculine and not all women are feminine. And most of us have been raised to believe that men date only women and women date only men. Clearly, this is not always the case.

Let's look at definitions of these three components:

**Gender Identity**   This is an individual's core conceptualization of himself or herself as male, female, or something in between. A person may express his or her gender identity as a transgendered person, transsexual, or intersexual (see the glossary at the end of this chapter for explanations of these terms).

**Sex Role Behavior**   This is behavior that can be categorized as "masculine" or "feminine" according to cultural norms. A person may express his or her sex role behavior as having a "male" or "female" sex role, being androgynous, or undifferentiated (see the glossary for explanations of these terms).

**Sexual Orientation**   This is the way an individual's sexual attractions are directed, that is, either toward the same sex, toward the opposite sex, toward both sexes, or toward neither sex. Sexual orientation may be determined by one's overt behavior, fantasies, or self-identification. Overt behaviors refer to sexual, affectional, and physical forms of intimacy with another person.

*Fantasies* refer to thoughts or daydreams one has about being intimate with another person. Self-identification refers to how a person describes his or her sexual orientation. It is important to understand

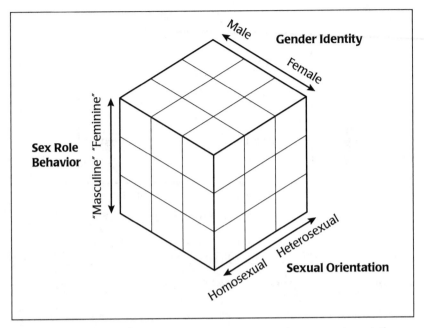

Three orientation categories generated by a three-dimensional model.

that a person does not need to have experienced any type of overt behavior before identifying his or her sexual orientation. There are many college students who have not been sexually active with another person but who strongly identify as having either same-sex or opposite-sex sexual orientation.

Money emphasizes that it's important to distinguish among the three components of sexual identity: gender identity, sex role behavior, and sexual orientation. It is easy to understand the three different components if you keep the following definitive questions in mind:

| | |
|---|---|
| *Gender identity:* | *"What sex do you feel like?"* |
| *Sex role behavior:* | *"What sex do you act like?"* |
| *Sexual orientation:* | *"What sex do you like?"* |

## Identifying Your Sexual Orientation
Sexual orientation has been described categorically and as existing along a continuum. Michael Storms (1980) portrays sexual orientation using a four-quadrant box:

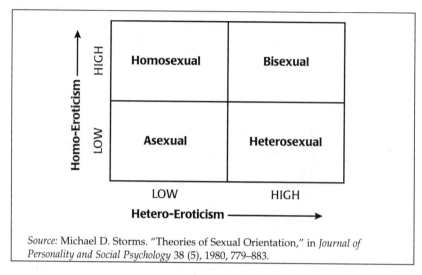

Source: Michael D. Storms. "Theories of Sexual Orientation," in *Journal of Personality and Social Psychology* 38 (5), 1980, 779–883.

Four orientation categories generated by a two-dimensional model.

In looking at different areas in Michael Storms's quadrants, we see that four expressions of sexual orientation identity are indicated. This approach to understanding sexual orientation focuses on a person's levels of homoeroticism and heteroeroticism. *Eroticism* means sexual excitement. As a person you can be low, medium, or high in one or both forms of eroticism. Your type (homo- or hetero-) and level of eroticism determine the nature of your sexual orientation.

One example is a person who is high in heteroeroticism and low in homoeroticism. This person may be described as being heterosexual. A second example is a person who is high in homoeroticism and low in heteroeroticism. This person may be described as being lesbian or gay. A final example is a person who is medium in both homoeroticism and heteroeroticism. This person may be described as being bisexual.

## Sexual Orientation Described Along a Continuum

Alfred Kinsey (1948, 1953), an American sociologist and biologist, interviewed hundreds of men and women about their sexual identity. Based on his conversations with men and women across the life span, Kinsey argued that sexual orientation existed on a continuum. From this belief, he created a seven-point scale that we now refer to as the Kinsey scale.

| 0 | 1 | 2 | 3 | 4 | 5 | 6 |
|---|---|---|---|---|---|---|
| Heterosexual | | | | | | Gay |

At the left end of the scale is the rank of 0. This represents a person whose behaviors, fantasies, and thoughts about sexual orientation identity are exclusively heterosexual in nature, whereas a rank of 1 refers to a person who is predominantly heterosexual and incidentally gay. At the right end of the scale is the rank of 6, which represents a person whose behaviors, fantasies, and thoughts about sexual orientation are exclusively gay or lesbian. In the middle of the scale is the rank of 3; it is believed that this person's behaviors, fantasies, and thoughts about sexual orientation are directed toward both sexes, that is, male and female. Historically, these persons have been referred to as being bisexual. These individuals are able to establish healthy, intimate relationships with either men or women. Kinsey thought that bisexuals were equally heterosexual and gay.

# Exercises on Understanding Your Sexual Identity

We have just learned about three components of sexual identity, Storms's four-quadrant categories for self-identifying one's sexual orientation, and Kinsey's 0–to–6 continuum scale. Now it's time for you to pause and reflect. Take a few minutes to complete the following exercises:

*Exercise 1. Answer the following questions.*

1. How would you describe your sexual identity? Use the four-quadrant box and think about where you see yourself in this regard.

2. How long have you been in this area of the box?

3. Do you think you will remain in this area of the box over the next 3 years? What about 5, 10, or even 15 years from now?

4. Where would you place yourself on the Kinsey scale?

    | 0 | 1 | 2 | 3 | 4 | 5 | 6 |
    |---|---|---|---|---|---|---|
    | Heterosexual | | | | | Gay | |

*Exercise 2. Answer the following questions.*

1. What sex do you feel like? (gender identity)

2. What sex do you act like? (sex role behavior)

3. What sex do you like? (sexual orientation)

It is important to note that the way you identify aspects of your sexual identity today may or may not be the same years from now. I want to emphasize that there is no right or wrong way to be. You are on a journey of self-discovery about your sexual identity.

## Sexual Identity and Heterosexual Assumptions

In her book *Understanding Sexual Identity: A Book for Gay and Lesbian Teens and Their Friends,* Janice Rench states:

> *Sexuality is a complex, fascinating subject, but one that many people don't feel comfortable discussing openly. There are many myths about homosexuality in particular. Unfortunately, most of these myths are degrading and describe gay people as abnormal, mentally ill, or dangerous to society. It is interesting to note that most of the people who believe these myths have never known any gay men or lesbians.*

The bleak and demoralizing images and messages we receive about gay, lesbian, and bisexual people fuel our prejudices and fears. We have learned that we should avoid these persons at all costs. We have also learned that it is okay—in fact even sporting—to ridicule and harass these individuals. Some people may think this is okay because, "After all, these people are different from us." They may even think things like "They choose to live this lifestyle" and "They bring this hardship on themselves by not being like the rest of us."

As we learn about sexual identity, we get many messages and images from society that shape what we believe. When we first encounter a man or a woman, we often automatically assign a gender identity to this person based on assumptions that are not always correct. Also, if a person fits our expectations about how we believe a man or a woman is supposed to act, walk, and talk, we automatically assign a particular sex role to this person. For example, we might say, "She is quite feminine," or "He is so masculine." And because a person looks like a man or a woman and acts as we expect, we assume that his or her sexual orientation is heterosexual. This assumption of heterosexuality complements the dominant messages and images of society.

Problems occur when a person does not look or act like a man or a woman in the eyes of others. When we internalize this perception of a person, we begin to question the person's sexual identity. We no longer automatically assume that this person fits the standard image of a heterosexual. It is at this point that our prejudices, fears, and discomfort take hold; our fear of the unknown is reinforced. Many of us will feel a strong need to avoid this person. We want this person to conform to mainstream acceptable ideas of gender identity, sex role behavior, and sexual orientation. In other words, we want this person to act as a heterosexual.

As a young adult in college, you will probably meet openly lesbian, gay, and bisexual persons. It is estimated that one in ten college students is lesbian, gay, or bisexual (Kinsey 1948). Therefore, if you attend a college that has 30,000 students, perhaps 3,000 or more students may be lesbian, gay, or bisexual. Let's say that your residence hall has 800 students; potentially, this means that 80 or more students may self-identify as being lesbian, gay, or bisexual.

How will you feel about and react to fellow students who are lesbian, gay, or bisexual? Will you feel prejudice, fear, or discomfort based upon the messages you learned from society? Or will you be able to set aside your fears and stereotypes? Will you be willing to keep an open mind and attempt to get to know these students? This is an important decision for you to consider as you begin to meet a unique group of students who identify themselves as lesbians, gays, or bisexuals.

# Lesbian, Gay, and Bisexual Students of Color

African American, Asian American, and Latin American lesbian, gay, and bisexual students have three aspects of their personal identity to manage during their college years. The first is being male or female. Men and women have different experiences in and outside the classroom. Many men generally feel more connected to male professors and are assumed to be more intelligent in comparison to women, whereas many women have talked about feeling invisible in the classroom and experiencing sexual harassment or discrimination from male professors.

The second aspect of personal identity is being non-white. Being an African American, Asian American, or Latin American student on a majority campus may often feel like being the only color dot within a sea of white. Sometimes students of color perceive responses and reactions from majority students and faculty that are based solely upon their skin color.

The third aspect of personal identity is being gay. To be different in this way from the mainstream heterosexual student and faculty population is often extremely difficult and troublesome. But it may also be a unique, special niche within the larger university community. Some gay students join organizations or support groups that meet their needs as lesbians, gays, and bisexuals. When gay students are provided the same freedom of expression and support systems afforded to heterosexual students, they are more likely to feel pride in themselves and their university.

## More Voices: Asian American Lesbians, Gay Men, and Bisexuals

These voices of Asian American lesbian, gay, and bisexual students reflect answers to questions about how family affects their gay identity, about being gay in a predominantly white gay community, and about having to choose between their racial/ethnic identity and their gay identity.

*"The family is your identity, and if you are rejected by the family you're isolated."*

—Anonymous (Wall and Washington 1991)

*"The gay community is so white and sometimes racist. I feel more comfortable with Asians and people of color."*

—Anonymous (Chan 1989)

*"I more strongly identify with the lesbian and gay identity [than my Asian identity] because I was politicized by my lesbianism and feminism."*

—Anonymous (Chan 1989)

*"[I identify with my identity as an] Asian American, because I can't deal with the white-dominated lesbian and gay scene. I guess I'm more race conscious than sexual-orientation conscious."*

—Anonymous (Chan 1989)

*"It is a problem to find my support only within the lesbian community, because I feel that I am either seen as 'exotic' and stereotyped, or unaccented because I am Asian and not like the majority of white lesbians."*

—Anonymous (Chan 1989)

*"While the Asian American community supports my Asian identity, the gay community only supports my being a gay man; as a result I find it difficult to identify with either."*

—Anonymous (Chan 1989)

# Coming Out

*Coming out* is defined as a process that gay individuals experience as they learn about being gay, lesbian, or bisexual. Coming out is a life-long journey toward self-discovery, self-acceptance, and self-love. Books such as Ann Heron's *One Teenager in Ten (1983)* and *Two Teenagers in Twenty* (1994) describe the challenges and struggles of coming-out experiences among lesbian, gay, and bisexual youth.

Even though the coming-out process may be turbulent, it is for many a quite positive experience. The two most difficult aspects of coming out are (1) being honest with one's self about one's sexual orientation, and (2) being honest with parents, siblings, friends, and significant other people (such as relatives and teachers) about one's sexual orientation.

In what is now a tradition, on October 11 of each year thousands of lesbian, gay, and bisexual college students celebrate National Coming Out Day. In the recent past, a group called Allies, most of whom are heterosexuals who affirm the rights of lesbian, gay, and bisexual people, also participated in this public celebration of pride. If we observe those who participate in this rally closely, we will generally see an almost totally white gay student and Allies audience. We are much less likely to see any noticeable presence of African American, Asian American, and Latin American lesbian, gay, and bisexual students or heterosexual Allies at this rally. This underscores the fact that coming out is often a quite different experience for gay students of color than it is for whites.

In a process similar to that of gay white students, many gay students of color experience difficulty accepting their own sexual orientation. When students of color first suspect that they're gay, they often attempt to deny this awareness. In order to further suppress it, they may date individuals of the opposite sex or place increased emphasis on academic and nonintimate social relationships. Students of color who are unsure about their sexual orientation may also go to great lengths to eradicate any behaviors, thoughts, or feelings that support their internal suspicions about being non-heterosexual. In general, this first part of the coming-out process, that is, being honest with oneself, is very similar for students of color and white gay students.

The second part of the coming out process, however—being honest with significant others about one's sexual orientation—is often more demanding and difficult for gay students of color. In fact, on predominantly white campuses, significant numbers of gay students of color choose to remain in the closet; to be out is just too risky. Wall and Washington (1991) state that "many lesbian and gay African Americans do not feel that coming out beyond themselves and other close gay and lesbian friends is necessary—or even smart."

For many reasons, gay students of color may share their sexual orientation with just a very few close friends. "Support networks are often small and private. Outside individuals are usually only brought into groups by already established members," commented one African American student (Wall and Washington 1991). Even to come out to other lesbian, gay, and bisexual individuals, gay students of color worry about gossip and exposure. A common fear among gay students of color is that if they come out publicly, they risk being shunned or outcast from one of their primary support networks—the African American, Asian American, Latin American community. For many lesbian, gay, and bisexual students of color, their racial/ethnic cultural community is highly important.

In interviews with Latina lesbians, Espin (1987) learned that they valued both aspects of their personal identity: being Latina and being lesbian. Latina lesbians experienced the fear of being stigmatized by their Latin community because of their sexual orientation. They also fear that the white lesbian, gay, and bisexual community will not offer them support around their identity as Latina women.

## Family Ties

Large numbers of college students maintain a strong bond with their family members, whose emotional, affectional, and financial support is invaluable. This family support gives students encouragement and motivation to deal with the problems associated with adjusting to college life.

Family support is also critical to lesbian, gay, and bisexual students of color. In some ways it may prove to be even more important than it is to straight heterosexual students. In general, racial and ethnic family systems place a high value on collaboration, cooperation, and interdependence. Oftentimes family members do all they can to take care of one another. Especially within a society that continues to oppress minority cultural groups, racial and ethnic families preach that in order to survive, the family must stick together. Therefore the gay student of color may feel a strong sense of kinship and obligation to his or her family.

Despite this strong family kinship and obligation, many gay students of color do not come out to their families. After interviewing Asian American lesbians and gay men, Chan pointed out that "in Asian cultures, being gay or lesbian is frequently viewed as a rejection of the most important roles for women and men—that of being a wife and mother for women and that of being a father carrying on the 'family line' [for men]" (Wall and Washington 1991). One Asian American student commented: "I wish I could tell my parents—they are the only ones who do not know about my gay identity, but I am sure that they would reject me. There is no frame of reference to understand homosexuality in a great number of Asian American cultures." In fact, in many Asian cultures (as well as other non-Western cultures) the terms *gay, lesbian,* and *bisexual* do not exist in their languages.

In upholding their responsibility to the family, gay students of color may believe that they must hide their sexual orientation from family members. As young boys and girls, gay students of color received explicit messages about appropriate gender and sex role behavior from their family. "Men don't cry" and "Women are to be ladies" are popular stereotypical expectations many parents hold for their sons and daughters. Therefore, the moment parents suspect that their child may be lesbian, gay, or bisexual, they immediately question their child's gender and sex role behaviors. In addition, parents often ask themselves, Where did we go wrong? Many parents then blame themselves for their child's sexual orientation and are confused about how to respond to their son or daughter in light of this new identity.

In addition, lesbian, gay, and bisexual students of color fear that they may lose the emotional, affectional, and financial support of their parents after they come out. They also worry that their siblings will find out about their sexual orientation. Because gay students of color are studying within a predominantly white campus environment and potentially confronting issues of racism, homophobia, and heterosexism, parental and family support becomes critical. To forfeit family support during these stressful times in one's life could possibly be just too much to ask of some closeted gay students of color.

# To the Parents of Gay Students of Color

*The family that loves and respects each other stays together.*

Discovering a son's or daughter's gay identity need not destroy the family's bond of love and respect. When the family learns about having a lesbian/bisexual daughter or a gay/bisexual son, four key areas of the family cultural systems may contribute to conflicts:

1. Religious values
2. Social expectations about marriage and reproduction
3. Gender and sex role expectations
4. External pressure from family, friends, or neighbors

If you as parents hold traditional religious values, expect marriage and grandchildren, and adhere to strict gender and sex role boundaries, you may feel you have to reject your gay/bisexual son or lesbian/bisexual daughter. However, it's important to consider reinterpreting your cultural world view. It may be possible for you to be flexible about maintaining your own cultural beliefs while permitting your unique son or daughter to create and establish his or her own beliefs, values, and norms. This flexibility reflects a loving bond and affirmation toward your child.

Within this posture of being flexible about your family cultural values, you as parents may still struggle to fully understand your gay son or daughter. You may ask yourself many questions: Why is my son gay? Why is my daughter a lesbian? What did we do as parents to cause our child to be this way? Were we good parents? It's important to not blame yourself. I do not know of any parents who asked to have a gay daughter or son. During this time it's important for you to say to yourself: I loved my child *before* I found out that he or she was gay—so why should that suddenly change? As parents, if you have a posture of flexibility, you can strengthen and maintain a positive relationship with your son or daughter.

## Coming Out to Parents

Why do daughters and sons come out to their parents? Gay youths give several powerful reasons for sharing their sexual orientation with one or both of their parents. One reason they cite is that they do not want to live a lie. Many find it increasingly difficult to hide their self-identity from the two most important people in their lives. Sneaking around with other gay friends while pretending to be at the library, at the arcade, or staying after school for a meeting can soon drain anyone's energy.

A second reason gay youth desire to come out to their parents is to gain support and reestablish a sense of closeness and intimacy. Many gay young people talk about feeling distant, isolated, and disconnected from their parents. Additionally, many experience feelings of guilt for being secretive. Lesbian, gay, and bisexual youth think to themselves: If I just tell them about my sexual orientation, we may be able to regain the closeness and intimacy in our relationship.

A final reason why gay students desire to come out to parents is to stop the bombardment of parental pressure about relationships with the opposite sex. Many gay youths tell stories about their parents going to extraordinary lengths to fix them up with potential husbands or wives. This form of pressure is also sometimes coupled with parents' desires for grandchildren. They may say, "Well, you know I'm not getting any younger and neither are you, so when are you going to give me some grandkids?" Again, some lesbian, gay, and bisexual individuals may feel mixed emotions. In the end, what troubles them most is the often profound guilt associated with not living up to parental expectations. For some, this guilt can be of disabling proportions.

# Gay, Lesbian, and Bisexual Student Groups and Organizations

On some predominantly white college and university campuses, support and resources for lesbian, gay, and bisexual students are becoming increasing visible. White lesbian, gay, and bisexual students are able to gather and discuss issues of importance to their personal development, political rights, and social welfare. Because sexual orientation is an invisible personal characteristic, gay students may assemble without heterosexual peers immediately recognizing why the group has gathered. In fact, even though many campus environments may be homophobic, the shield that often protects white gay students is their skin color, which helps them blend in to the larger predominantly white institutional community.

On the other hand, just because gay student organizations exist on predominantly white campuses, gay students of color may not feel comfortable joining these groups and may even consciously avoid them. Gay students of color are presented with a different set of challenges and choices in deciding what type of organizations to join. As a visible racial or ethnic group member on a white campus, gay students of color may already feel separated from the larger white campus community. As a gay student of color, you may feel that you are "in a fishbowl," considering that there are so few students of color on your campus. You may even feel compelled to join an organization that focuses on your needs and experiences as a student of color.

But then, on the other hand, as a gay student of color, you will probably want to meet and interact with other gay students. So what do you need to think about before deciding to join a predominantly white gay support organization? You think to yourself: I'm sure to stand out, since I'll be the only "color fish" at the gathering. Also, you realize that white students are often acutely aware of when African American, Asian American, or Latin American students join or leave any type of meeting or gathering.

So gay students of color ask themselves whether they would feel comfortable joining a predominantly white student organization or support group. They may wonder if such a group will meet their needs as racial/ethnic individuals. Very often these students report experiencing prejudice and racism within predominantly white gay organizations. In the face of this dilemma, some may decide to remain in the closet and to keep strong ties to their racial/ethnic community. In making this decision, gay students of color do not get support for their identity as gay individuals. Another reaction to this dilemma is that many gay students of color choose to participate in gay-related events away from their college campus so that their racial/ethnic community will not find out about their sexual orientation.

# Final Voices: Latin American Lesbians, Gay Men, and Bisexuals

*"There's a special kind of attachment to the masculine and the female in our culture. It makes it more difficult to be self-accepting."*
—Anonymous (Wall and Johnson 1991)

*"I am so afraid that my Hispanic friends will tell my family that I am gay. Our families are so connected. I meet my family every Sunday for dinner at*

*Grandma's—and every Sunday I meet a new family member who knows someone on my campus."*
—Anonymous (Wall and Johnson 1991)

*"I knew whatever I was doing wasn't right and that I was going to hell for sure." [Latin American gay student commenting on religious beliefs.]*
—Anonymous (Wall & Johnson, 1991)

## Brothers and Sisters in the Life

It may be possible to get involved with a small, informal student-of-color gay community group. There a few predominantly white campuses on which African American, Asian American, and Latin American lesbian, gay, and bisexual students have formed their own unique support network. Some gay students of color, however, feel that they are not able to choose one aspect of their personal identity— racial/ethnic or sexual orientation—over another. For these students, support and acceptance from both their racial/ethnic cultural community and the white gay community are important.

### Becoming Aware of Yourself: Racial and Sexual Orientation Identity Development

How do you know which support networks will meet your needs? Your college experience represents an opportunity for you to learn about your academic and career interests, enhance your interpersonal skills and relationships, and increase your level of self-understanding as a person. Specifically, from interviews with African American, Asian American, and Latin American lesbian, gay, and bisexual students, two major cultural aspects of personal identity seem to stand out.

The first is racial/ethnic identity, which represents a *visible* cultural characteristic that makes African American, Asian American, or Latin American students distinct from white students. The second aspect is sexual orientation identity. Being lesbian, gay, or bisexual represents a distinct *invisible* cultural characteristic that makes African American, Asian American, or Latin American students distinct from all heterosexual students, both white and of color. Many student affairs professionals recognize the importance of both the racial identity development process and the lesbian, gay, and bisexual development process experienced by students.

Racial identity development has been described as a process by which a student of color develops an ongoing and heightened awareness of his or her racial/ethnic cultural background and its level of importance and meaning. Students of color also begin to reflect upon how mainstream society responds to them as being distinct racial/ethnic individuals. As a student of color coming from perhaps a culturally mixed community and high school, your racial identity may not have been of much concern. Now, as a student of color on a predominantly white campus, your racial identity may become a concern since you are now seen as being a member of a minority group.

Racial identity models suggest that as students of color you may experience periods when your racial identity is the most critical aspect of your personal identity. You may place a high value on being connected with your own racial/ethnic group, on having a perspective that incorporates the realities of your own racial/ethnic group experiences, and perhaps on devaluing the majority white culture. Yet, later in the growth process, you may experience a feeling of genuine pride about your own cultural heritage while also accepting some white cultural group members and perspectives. During the racial identity development process, the level of importance assigned to your racial identity increases as the range of your social and cultural experiences increases.

In a similar vein, gay identity development is a process by which you develop an ongoing awareness of yourself as being lesbian, gay, or bisexual. You also may begin to think about how people may treat you if they knew you were not a heterosexual. Many individuals become aware of their sexual orientation as an adolescent in high school or a young adult in college. If you recognize that your physical, affectional, emotional, and sexual attractions and intimate and romantic interests are toward members of the same sex or both sexes, this may be an alarming and shocking awareness for you, especially if for most of your life you have thought or assumed that you were heterosexual. Initially, as far as you know, all of your parents, siblings, aunts and uncles, cousins, and student peers are heterosexual. It is also a potentially shocking realization because as you reflect on your understanding of how society treats gay people, you know that they are not highly valued or accepted in most segments of society.

This initial phase in understanding your sexual identity may feel quite confusing, fearful, and painful. Lesbian, gay, and bisexual identity models suggest that there are periods when you may want to deny or downplay your growing self-awareness of being gay. During this period you may make comparisons between the experiences of heterosexual members of society and stereotypical or known experiences of lesbian, gay, or bisexual people.

Hopefully, there will come a period when you are able to accept and appreciate your sexual orientation identity. Many gay individuals encounter intense feelings of pride about their sexual orientation while devaluing heterosexuals and heterosexual values, attitudes, and behavioral norms. This would be a normal feeling for you to experience. In latter periods of the gay identity process, however, you may have both positive and negative feelings about the gay community and the heterosexual community. It's important to realize that the level of significance assigned to your sexual identity generally increases as the range of your social and cultural experiences increases.

## We Are Family: Being an Ally of the Gay Community

This final section focuses on the commonalties among us all—gay students of color, gay white students, and heterosexual non-white and white students.

If we are to foster a more empathic and understanding culturally diverse community on campus, we each must take responsibility for supporting and respecting one another. To be lesbian, gay, bisexual, or heterosexual is not a crime. To be African American, Asian American, Latin American, Native American, or white American is not a crime. What is wrong is to dismiss or prejudge a fellow student by some personal qualities that do not necessarily have anything to do with the person's character.

In particular, heterosexual students may play a significant role in the lives of lesbian, gay, and bisexual students. Even though we all enjoy being around and hanging out with people who are like us, we also find pleasure in being with and learning about people who are different. As a heterosexual student, you can be an Ally—a person who supports and affirms the experiences and lives of lesbian, gay, and bisexual people. But, as a heterosexual student, you may wonder: Why should I be supportive of gay students? To help you consider this, think about how you would answer the following questions:

1. When was the first time you discovered that you were a heterosexual?

2. When was the first time you realized that you were attracted to the opposite sex?

3. Did you run to your parents and tell them, "Mom and Dad, guess what? I am heterosexual!"

4. Did you feel the need to tell your siblings that you were heterosexual?

5. Did you wonder how students in school would react if you told them you were heterosexual?

6. Did you wonder how everyone would react if you held hands with a person of the opposite sex?

7. Did you wonder how everyone would react if you went on a date with a person of the opposite sex?

8. Did you wonder if your teachers and the principal would let you attend the high school prom when they discovered that you were heterosexual?

9. When was the last time you felt that you could not tell your doctor, employer, minister, or best friend that you were heterosexual?

10. When was the last time you read graffiti saying: "Kill all heterosexuals!"

My guess is that as a heterosexual individual, you have not had to consciously think about any of these questions. I may be wrong. Am I? Unfortunately, lesbian, gay, and bisexual students have to think about most of these questions virtually all of their lives. How might you feel if you had to think about these questions almost every day? Would you feel liked? Would you feel appreciated? Would you feel happiness? Would you feel loved? My guess is that you would feel disliked, unappreciated, unhappy, and unloved. In our society almost all lesbian, gay, and bisexual people have experienced these emotions and feelings, especially when they first discovered that they might not be heterosexual.

Now, what would you feel today, at this very moment, if someone said to you, "You are gay. We know that for many years you thought you were heterosexual. We just didn't think you could handle the truth until now." Imagine the shock. Imagine the fear. Imagine the sense of extreme confusion. Imagine losing a known identity. Imagine yourself having all of these strong, and many times conflicting, feelings.

If you were able to make this role reversal that I just led you through, perhaps you can begin to understand what lesbian, gay, and bisexual students may feel *at different times* in their lives. I want to emphasize *at different times*, because many lesbian, gay, and bisexual students do develop a positive and self-loving attitude toward themselves and their sexual orientation. What adds to their level of comfort and affirmation is having the support and respect of heterosexual students who take the role of an Ally. You need to decide if the foregoing argument is compelling enough for you to become an Ally. Many find it so, and I hope that you will, too.

# Glossary of Terms Related to Chapter 10

**Ally**  Any person who is not a lesbian, gay man, or bisexual, whose attitudes and behaviors are antiheterosexist in perspective and who works toward combating homophobia and heterosexism, both on a personal and institutional level.

**androgynous**  Having a number of characteristics that can be described as masculine, as well as a number of characteristics that can be described as feminine.

**bisexual**  A common and acceptable term for a woman or man who is primarily emotionally, physically, or sexually attracted or committed to a member or members of the same gender, and emotionally, physically, or sexually attracted or committed to a member or members of the opposite gender. A bisexual person may be attracted to both a member of the opposite or of the same gender at the same time.

**coming out**  To come out is to affirm and declare publicly one's lesbian, gay, or bisexual identity—sometimes to one person in conversation, sometimes by an act that places one in the public eye. It is not an isolated event, but a lifelong process. In each new situation, a lesbian, gay man, or bisexual person must decide whether or not to come out.

**cross-dresser**  Someone who wears clothes typically associated with the opposite sex. People cross-dress for a variety of reasons, which may or may not be directly associated with gender identity, sex role behavior, or sexual orientation. A person who engages in cross-dressing may identify as heterosexual, lesbian, gay, or bisexual.

**eroticism**   Sexual excitement.

**erotophobia**   Fear of or discomfort with one's own sexuality.

**familismo**   The importance of the family as the primary social unit and source of support in the Latin culture. The extended family is intimately and actively involved.

**gay**   A common and acceptable term for someone who is primarily emotionally, physically, or sexually attracted or committed to a member or members of the same gender. This term is more frequently attributed to a man than to a woman.

**gender identity**   An individual's core conceptualization of himself or herself as male, female, or some combination of these characteristics. A person may express his or her gender identity as a transgendered person, transsexual, or intersexual.

**gender role**   An overall constellation of sex role behaviors that add up to a "male sex role" or a "female sex role" within a given culture.

**heterosexism**   Sexual orientation prejudice plus the backup of institutional power to impose that prejudice, used to the advantage of one group with a particular sexual orientation and to the disadvantage of another. Heterosexism is any attitude, action, or institutional action—backed up by institutional power—that subordinates people because of their sexual orientation; that is, the expectation and assumption that everyone is heterosexual.

**heterosexual**   A person who is primarily emotionally, physically, or sexually attracted or committed to a member or members of the opposite sex.

**homophobia**   The irrational fear of gay men or lesbians, or any behavior, belief, or attitude toward yourself or others that does not conform to rigid gender role stereotypes. Homophobia is the fear that enforces sexism as well as heterosexism. The extreme behavior of homophobia is violence against gay men and lesbians.

**homosexual**   A person (lesbian or gay man) who is primarily emotionally, physically, or sexually attracted or committed to a member or members of the same gender. This term is archaic, clinical, offensive, and unacceptable to many people. *Gay man, gay woman,* or *lesbian* is more acceptable.

**in the closet**   To hide one's lesbian, gay, or bisexual identity and to pretend to be heterosexual; to "pass" and live a fragmented identity in order to keep a job, a housing situation, friends, or to in some other way survive. Many gay people are "out" in some situations and "closeted" in others.

**institutional oppression**  Institutional arrangements of a society used to benefit one group at the expense of another. Institutional oppression is typically carried out through religion, education, government, or business.

**internalized oppression by lesbians/gay men/bisexuals**  The adoption and acceptance within a lesbian, gay man, or bisexual that negative attitudes and beliefs about lesbians, gay men, and bisexuals are true.

**intersexual**  An individual with ambiguous biological sex. Less accurately referred to as a hermaphrodite.

**lesbian**  A common and acceptable term for a woman who is primarily emotionally, physically, or sexually attracted or committed to other women. *Gay woman* is also an acceptable term; however, some women prefer to be called *lesbians*, because in today's society the term gay generally refers to men. The term *lesbian* gives gay women their own identity.

**machismo**  The responsibility of a Latino man to provide, protect, and defend his family. It is his loyalty and sense of responsibility to his family, friends, and community that makes him a man and this is reflected in his *machismo*. This is entirely different from the Anglo view of macho as connoting sexist, male chauvinist behavior.

**queer**  A term used by the gay community to identify lesbians, gay men, and bisexual individuals; selected to indicate self-determinism and provide one word to describe the gay community. This term has often been associated with political ideology.

**sex role behavior**  Behavior that can be categorized as masculine or feminine, according to cultural norms. A person may express his or her sex role behavior as having a male or female sex role, being androgynous, or undifferentiated.

**sexual orientation**  The way an individual's sexual attractions are directed, that is, either toward the same sex, toward the opposite sex, toward both sexes, or toward neither sex. Sexual orientation may be determined by one's overt behavior, fantasies, or self-identification. Overt behaviors refer to sexual, affectional, and physical forms of intimacy with another person.

**transsexual**  A transgendered individual who has chosen to live as a member of the sex opposite from that to which he or she was born.

**transgendered**   Having a core sense of gender identity that is at odds with one's biological sex.

**transvestite**   A man who dresses as a woman on a regular basis, often as an erotic act. Such a person may or may not be transgendered.

**undifferentiated**   Having few characteristics that can be characterized as either masculine or feminine.

**xenophobia**   Discomfort with one's differentness.

# References

Chan, C. S. "Issues of Identity Development Among Asian American Lesbians and Gay Men," in *Journal of Counseling and Development* 68, 1989, 16–20.

Epsin, O. M. (1987). "Issues of Identity in the Psychology of Latina Lesbians," in Boston Lesbian Psychologies Collective (Ed.), *Lesbian psychologies: Explorations and challenges* (pp. 35–51). Urbana: University of Illinois Press.

Heron, Ann, ed. *One Teenager in Ten: Writings by Gay and Lesbian Youth* (Boston: Alysons Publications, 1983).

Heron, Ann, ed. *Two Teenagers in Twenty: Writings by Gay and Lesbian Youth* (Boston: Alysons Publications, 1994).

Hoyenga, K. B. & Hoyenga, K. T. (1993). *Gender-Related Differences: Orgins and Outcomes.* Needham Heights, MA: Allyn and Bacon.

Johnson, J. M. (1981). Influence of assimilation on the psychological adjustment of Black homosexual men. Unpublished doctoral dissertation, California School of Professional Psychology, Berkeley, CA.

Kinsey, A., Pomeroy, W. B., & Martin, C. E. (1948). *Sexual behavior in the human male.* Philadelphia: W. B. Saunders.

Kinsey, A., Pomeroy, W. B., Martin, C. E., & Gebhard, P. H. (1953). *Sexual behavior in the human female.* Philadelphia: W. B. Saunders.

Loiacano, D. K. "Gay Identity Issues Among Black Americans: Racism, Homophobia, and the Need for Validation," in *Journal of Counseling and Development* 68, 1989, 21–25.

Money, J. (1986). *Venuses penuses: Sexology, sexosophy, and exigency theory.* Buffalo, New York: Prometheus Books.

Rench, Janice E. *Understanding Sexual Identity: A Book for Gay and Lesbian Teens and Their Friends* (Minneapolis: Lerner Publications, 1990).

Wall, V. A., and J. Washington. "Understanding Gay and Lesbian Students of Color," in N. J. Evans and V. A. Wall, *Beyond Tolerance: Gays, Lesbians, and Bisexuals on Campus* (Alexandria, Va.: American Association for Counseling and Development, 1991), 67–78.

## Resources

Chan, C. S. "Cultural Considerations in Counseling Asian American Lesbians and Gay Men," in S. H. Dworkin and F. J. Gutierrez, eds., *Counseling Gay Men and Lesbians: Journey to the End of the Rainbow* (Alexandria, Va.: American Association for Counseling and Development, 1992), 115–124.

Elkins, J. B., and H. L. Sjoberg. *Language and Definitions Regarding People Who Are Lesbian/Gay/Bisexual*, training workshop, 1991.

Evans, N. J., and V. A. Wall. *Beyond Tolerance: Gays, Lesbians, and Bisexuals on Campus* (Alexandria, Va.: American Association for Counseling and Development, 1991).

Gutierrez, F. J., and S. H. Dworkin. "Gay, Lesbian, and African American: Managing the Integration of Identities," in S. H. Dworkin and F. J. Gutierrez, eds., *Counseling Gay Men and Lesbians: Journey to the End of the Rainbow* (Alexandria, Va.: American Association for Counseling and Development, 1992), 141–156.

Monterio, K. P., and V. Fuqua. "African American Gay Youth: One Form of Manhood," in *The High School Journal* 77 (1) and 77 (2), 1994, 20–36.

Morales, E. S. "Counseling Latino Gays and Latina Lesbians," in S. H. Dworkin and F. J. Gutierrez, eds., *Counseling Gay Men and Lesbians: Journey to the End of the Rainbow* (Alexandria, Va.: American Association for Counseling and Development, 1992), 125–139).

Wolf, T. J. "Bisexuality: A Counseling Perspective," in S. H. Dworkin and F. J. Gutierrez, eds., *Counseling Gay Men and Lesbians: Journey to the End of the Rainbow* (Alexandria, Va.: American Association for Counseling and Development, 1992), 175–187.

# Chapter 11

# Fifteen International Students of Color Discuss Their Experiences at PWIs

### Wanjuri Kamau

This chapter presents the voices of fifteen international students of color studying in the United States from the following eight countries: China, Ethiopia, India, Indonesia, Kenya, Nigeria, Taiwan, and Tanzania. At the time of the interviews, all were attending school at various predominantly white institutions (PWIs) in the United States. These are their stories, reflecting their journeys as they embarked on a college education away from their home countries. They are stories of changing, learning, and adapting to the challenges of college life for international students. Collectively, their stories present a shared goal within their families—the desire for a college education and the search for a better tomorrow. These stories reflect different behaviors and ways of thinking that are shaped by diverse cultures, values, and beliefs. These are voices of how international students mediate change, individually or collectively, within the American education system and culture.

## Interview Background

The group that was interviewed consisted of eight males and seven females, and their median age was twenty-two. One student was a freshman, four were in their sophomore year, seven were juniors, and three were seniors. Fourteen lived on campus for at least one year; one lived off campus with her aunt.

A semistructured questionnaire aided in obtaining information from the students. The topics covered included identifying information about who the students were within their sociocultural context, how they applied and prepared themselves for their college education, their expectations and college experiences, and their advice to other new international students of color who hoped to attend predominantly white institutions.

The names used here are pseudonyms to protect the identities of the students interviewed. The information, however, is real and represents the students' college experiences. Most of the quotations are excerpts from verbal responses to the structured questions, which were generated from specified themes characterized in other chapters of this book. Finally, please note that some answers were omitted to avoid repetition.

# Similarities Among the Students

The interviews with the participating international students revealed many similarities among them. These similarities are as follows:

- ✔ Based on their grade-point averages (GPAs), the interviewees appeared to be very bright students who excelled in their meritorious systems of education strictly based on performance. The students reported education in their home countries as very competitive and limited in terms of choice of study area. Stringent examinations and qualifications admitted relatively few students, while the demand for college graduates was very high. The lowest level of academic performance in the group of interviewees was 3.50 (on the standard scale of 4.00).

- ✔ The parents' socioeconomic groups ranged from middle to upper class in their home countries.

- ✔ None of the students interviewed thought of themselves as minorities or students of color before coming to the United States.

- ✔ All of the students had strong family ties and support that extended beyond the Western nuclear family unit. All stressed roots over individualism. As a result, their coming to the United States for education was a shared goal of the students, their teachers, and their extended families.

- ✔ All of the students interviewed regarded elders and people of authority, such as teachers, with high respect.

- ✔ English was the second language of all students. Each had to pass TOEFL or SAT exams before admission to the American universities.

- ✔ All students had to show bank drafts as proof that their parents could afford to pay for out-of-state tuition, room and board, books, personal expenses, and health insurance for four years. These students were not eligible for federal government grants and were not allowed to work in the United States. In some cases, work on campus could be negotiated with the foreign students office after completion of one academic year.

✔ All of the students interviewed followed the English system of education with slight variations. This common heritage has roots in colonization by Britain.

✔ In order to travel, each student had to secure a passport from his or her country of origin and a visa from the United States. The U.S. visa was issued to students only after they submitted Form 1-20, which was taken as proof by the U.S. embassies that all admission requirements had been met.

# Cultural Backgrounds of Students

Each interviewee was asked to briefly describe him- or herself and his or her home, country, and culture. They were also asked if they lived in an urban or rural setting and in an industrialized or non-industrialized country. Their responses follow.

### Oyewu, a student from rural Nigeria

"I remember my childhood with nostalgia; I did most of my work in daylight, because there was no light at night. Reading with a lantern did not bother me, but if we did not have paraffin oil, it meant that I would not study, so I tried to do all my homework during the day to avoid uncontrollable inconveniences. That way I also had time to play at night in the moonlight with other children in my neighborhood. I really looked forward to the nights where playing was okay and not marred with other chores, as was the case during the day after school. I also attended school in town and lived with my uncle during school time and went home during the holiday.... I read anything I could get my hands on. I read the Bible most, and the Koran because my uncle was a Muslim. I preferred the village though, because all my friends lived together. That was not so at my uncle's house. When my father came back from America after one year's stay, he said he would teach us himself, and I did not have to go to the city again."

### Helina, from Ethiopia

"I grew up in rural Ethiopia. We were six in the family. My father was a high school graduate and my mother had primary school education. Going to school was not a choice—it was a chore, like washing dishes; and not only did we have to go to school, we had to perform well. When you wash dishes, you have to rinse the soap well and with great care so that people do not taste the soap. My mother was very particular about cleaning the dishes well, and that is the childhood chore that left a great impact on me. My mother's job was to ensure that she made food for us, and my father paid the school fees. Our duty as children was to study and do well at school. My parents would always emphasize the importance of being honest in everything including our thoughts. My grandparents lived with us and when we did well in school every one knew, including the neighbors. They also knew when we did not do well in school, and it was very embarrassing. I felt like I let everybody down and that was a heavy burden to bear. There was no electricity in my village, and we had a communal tap of water, where most women met and exchanged gossip and other news. We cooked with charcoal, and lighting charcoal was difficult during the rainy season. My parents would always tell us to study hard so that we could move to town, where there are better facilities. I am working hard to offer a better life to my parents and my village. This commitment is what keeps me going. They have sacrificed so much for me to be here; my parents and the villagers collectively raised money for me to come to the United States."

### Furaha, from Moshi, a rural area in Tanzania

"I lived in the same compound with my grandparents, uncles, and their families. Although my parents were economically better off than my neighbors, we all did not have electricity or running water. We used a donkey to draw water from the river, but others in the area carried it on their heads. For my primary education, I attended a private parochial school run by nuns; I walked back and forth to school. I attended a government-aided high school after excelling in my primary school terminal examinations. There were two of us who passed to go to secondary school in my village, and my parents were very proud of me. I was also proud of myself for fulfilling their wishes that I work hard in school. The high school was away from home. I went home only during the holidays."

### Ghai, from India

"My brother and I grew up in the suburbs of New Delhi and attended a private kindergarten and primary school. My grandparents lived with us. My parents had two cars, and we each had two bicycles while growing up. Actually, my life was not any different from that of any other kid living in the suburbs of other cities in the world."

## Commentary

Oyewu's comments in particular are a reflection of a widely held belief in many countries, developed and developing, that urban schools are better than schools in rural areas. A father, who wanted to send his son to the United States for college, obviously took upon himself the task of educating him in his early years.

An interesting observation about the settings described is that whether in town or not, the characteristic of extended family and commitment to roots was maintained. The grandparents taught the younger generation the language and the traditions. The parents taught their children the modern ways. The teachers enjoyed special positions, because they held the power of the books. For example, in Nigeria and Kenya, to read books is the highest calling—it means learning to read, study, and gain access to the fruits of hard-won political independence; it means getting on with life.

# Choice of a Predominantly White Institution

The students interviewed were asked how they chose predominantly white institutions, and replied as follows.

### Karamshi, from Indonesia

"My father wanted me to go to college abroad to fulfill his own unsuccessful desire to study engineering abroad. My uncle had attended college in Ohio, and he advised me to choose schools that were in rural settings as opposed to institutions in urban areas. I went to the U.S. embassy in Jakarta and requested a list of engineering colleges in the United States. They gave me a list of three thousand accredited colleges, which I narrowed down to ten, according to their ratings and physical environment. Penn State University was among the top ten. Although I was not looking for people like myself, I noticed that there were Indians on the faculty, and that was a surprise but pleasing. The decision was between Penn State and Ohio State, and I chose PSU because it was better in many ways. It also happens that PSU processed my application faster than any other college."

Karamshi's parents are successful Chinese industrialists who live in Jakarta, the capital of Indonesia. Karamshi attended a private international high school in Singapore with students from many parts of the world. He left home to live in a private boarding school when he was eleven years old. During school holidays he worked in his father's business.

### Kabede, whose parents are college professors in Ethiopia

"I knew that America was predominantly white, and race was not therefore an issue for me. What my parents and I were after was a good institution that offered a difference from the Ethiopian institutions. I wanted to study materials science and I was looking for a college that was good, not who attended the college. My parents had studied here and they helped me locate a small private institution on the East Coast of the United States. They considered small institutions better than big institutions, because a student gets individual attention. The individual attention prepares one well for graduate education, which is my next goal."

### Oyewu, from Nigeria

"My brother was already attending a private institution in the south of the United States where my father had been a student. The family collective criteria for universities was that it had to offer fine education and nothing else. My father taught me how to pronounce words whose meanings are the same but which are pronounced or spelled differently in American English, like *schedule, favor [favour], color [colour], behavior [behaviour],* and *center [centre].* He also helped me study the SAT, which is culturally biased."

Oyewu's father had spent one year of education in the United States on an exchange program for teachers between the United States and Nigeria. Oyewu stated that his father was determined to educate his children under the U.S. system of education, which he admired during his one-year stay.

### Mumbi, from Kenya, whose mother is a successful businesswoman

"It was my aunt who was working in the United States who chose the school for me. I had attended a high school with students from all over the globe in Nairobi, which is a metropolitan city and the home of many United Nations offices like UNEP and UNDP. At the time, the University of Nairobi, which I wanted to attend and study law, had been closed indefinitely by the government to quell student demonstrations. I was happy and considered myself very fortunate to have a school when my colleagues in Kenya did not. I was not able to study law, because in America law is studied after the first degree, and at home you go straight to your major field as an undergraduate. While I regretted my inability to enter law, the American system has provided me with a sound liberal arts education which I think will make me a better lawyer when I go home or to England for law training next year. I was shocked by the differentiation of students on color lines. Above all I was disgusted by the way some students and teachers address me as a nonentity; a minor, that is my interpretation of minority—a person who is less than an adult. This reaction to labeling me on skin color has challenged me to prove that I am not what they think— I am not a minor brain-wise-by achieving a GPA of 3.91. If it had not been for one professor who has refused to give me an A, I would be having a GPA of 4.00. I work very hard, but the English professor does not believe that non-English speakers, especially Africans, can master the language. I shared with him a list of world-renowned literature writers from Kenya and Nigeria, and he admitted having no knowledge of their work. I feel angry because English literature had been my best subject throughout high school, and I even made a distinction pass in my 'O level' examinations."

### Sheng, from China

"Computer technology has always interested me, and I was looking for a school where I could study and master it in order to write my own computer program. I was good in physics and mathematics; and my father, who is an electrical engineer, helped me through the American embassy at home to secure a place at PSU, which was recommended by a professor who was my father's customer. The quality of education was what we were looking for and it did not matter where the institution was located and who attended it."

### Ghai, from India, whose father is a mechanical engineer and whose mother is a psychologist

"The question of predominantly white institutions did not arise. I had studied geography and I knew that the inhabitants of North America were predominantly white. One thing was certain to me anyway—that the people and their culture would be different from my Indian one. I had been in the United States as a tourist with my parents three times before coming here, and had observed the flexibility of education provided by American universities and admired it. My parents, on the other hand, earned their degrees from Britain, and their desire was for me to go to Cambridge University in England. They considered English education more prestigious than American education. I did very well in my terminal examinations and was accepted to go to Cambridge University, but my mind was set to come to the United States. I had it in a strict private high school in India, which was modeled under the English public schools. The American embassy in Delhi helped me by giving me a list of top engineering schools on the East Coast near my uncle who lives in New Jersey. Penn State was one of them and I applied. I was accepted at Penn State, and my parents paid the stipulated expenses when they realized that Penn State is one of the best institutions in engineering. The United States Education Foundation of India (USEFI), which included PSU alumni as well as currently enrolled students, gave us a two-day orientation. They showed us a video of Boston University as a typical American university, and the majority of students were white. My younger brother followed me one year after."

### Nina, from Taiwan

"My college choice had to be close to a relative and had to provide a small student ratio (4 to 1). It had to be in the top ten schools of journalism. My parents are professionals and they wanted the best for me."

### Commentary

It was clear from the answers that good education was what the students and their families wanted from the United States. The issue of skin color did not feature in the students' decisions when choosing an institution. As a matter of fact, several of them laughed at the question, implying that, from their point of view, education and skin color did not correlate. It was also true that all of them had attended diverse high schools in their home countries, where they had grown accustomed to diversity. Their parents' way of looking at the world and the diversity in their high schools and communities helped to explain that their views of the world would have to be open and more inclusive.

## Students' Reasons for Attending College

When asked to describe why they were in college, the interviewed students had the following responses.

### Oyewu, from Nigeria

"I am attending college so that I can help my village in Nigeria to combat the health problems that face us. For example, where my grandmother lives, not all people have running water in their homes, and I

More and more Asian students are entering college with many different attitudes and values.

am studying engineering to learn more efficient ways of accessing water. College for me is not a choice—it is a duty for my people. Besides, it is clear that our parents expect all of us to attend college, and my duty is to obey what they tell me, that is also my joy."

Asked to elaborate about parental duty, Oyewu said that in her culture children are taught that since their parents gave them life, they owe their life to their parents, and appreciation is measured by obedience. The obedience, in turn, gives them joy because their parents are happy with them.

### Ghai, from India

"College education is the key to success. I want to open a successful financial business between India and the United States, where the Indian currency is respected."

### Karamshi, from Indonesia

"I am in college to fulfill my father's dream. My father wanted to study abroad and he did not. He was determined to send me abroad so that I can be in a better position to take over the family business. I owe him my life and it gives me pleasure to make my parents happy."

### Mumbi, from Kenya

"College means job security and prestige. I want to be a leader like our vice president. He graduated from Harvard in the sixties. My home is near his, and I am determined to succeed him in Parliament. I know I will achieve my goal, because I work hard in school and my grades bear witness to my goal."

### Sheng, from Taiwan

"I did not have to think about college. It is a matter of course to get at least graduate education in my family."

### Nina, from Taiwan

"I was gunshot on getting an American experience and did all I could to shield myself away from hanging out too much with people from Taiwan. It was the only way to improve my spoken English in order to excel in journalism. My parents support me, as they believe education is key to success. As a result, they pay my upkeep as well as the tuition. All I have to do is go to school and perform well."

### Furaha, from Tanzania

"Passing all the examinations well left me no choice—I was college bound. Everybody knew it; passing well means going on with school. University of Dar-es-Salaam and the Agricultural College in Moshi did not offer computer science. People got together and raised money for me to come to America. I believe that God gave me a talent not to keep but to share with others. So, since not everyone is academically able to go to college, I am determined to finish and go home to help those who sent me here."

### Commentary

All fifteen of the students interviewed had a clear vision of college education and placed a high priority on it. They indicated a natural pursuit of education that was rooted in their family, relatives, and friends and sometimes on the much bigger scale of their country's needs. The students' commitment to education is demonstrated by their willingness to leave the comfort and security of their familiar homes to seek what was not available in their country.

It was also clear that the academic undertaking was a shared endeavor among the parents who financed the education, the teachers, the extended family, and the students who performed well to ensure success. In this sense, the student's success became communal. The students approached their education with a mindset of academic success that would match or surpass that of their parents. This clear vision was the guiding force toward commitment to graduation.

It is customary in many cultures to share costs among different parties for important events, including education, weddings, and funeral ceremonies. The popular saying that "It takes a village to raise a child" is personified in the instance of the people in Furaha's village raising money for her to go to college in the United States. Contributing resources, no matter the value, is indicative of the commitment the village community has toward its members.

# Student Expectations of Institutions

Students were asked to evaluate their expectations of the institutions they attended and how well those expectations were met. The responses follow.

### Nila, from India

"I expected a more rigid system of education than the one I found. I find the students disrespectful to their professors. The students are too free and the professors are too easy. I expected school to be difficult but I find it easy. I do not have to work as hard as in India. In fact, I study fewer hours in college than I did in high school and find time to read novels and watch television."

### Nina, from Taiwan

"I expected challenges and accepted them as my responsibility for better career opportunities."

### Ghai, from India

"I expected the Americans to be more informed about India and countries other than the United States. Students often ask me whether we have cars in India. And some students and professors are amazed that I can speak English and wonder how I learned the language. I expected professors to know some history about India and its relationship with Britain as a colony. Generally, I am happier that I came to school here, because my opinion is respected. When I ask professors how come they do not know Indian history, they take no offense—a thing which would cost a student their presence in school in India, as it would be considered rude. I am getting more than I expected and I have become more assertive."

### Aidoo, from Nigeria

"I did not expect to be known as a minority. I still do not think anybody should label me a minority just because of my skin color. I expected to face no injustices purely on the basis of my skin color. What I had learned about the American Constitution had filled my mind with true democracy, but now I do not think there is anything like that. It is all words."

### Karamshi, from Indonesia

"I expected to be accepted and respected as I was back home. In Jakarta everyone knew my father and respected us. The International school and the American embassy in Jakarta painted the college experience in America enjoyable and inclusive. For some reason I did not think there was any difference between me and the white students worth noticing in the orientation video that I and other students saw in Jakarta. The skin color is basic, it is a given, I thought. The difference I thought would be in our performances, and I had them well taken care of in passing with honors. Nobody told me that America is run on color lines. I did not expect to find the color issue a preoccupation of the magnitude the newspapers say it is. My expectations of America has changed and I am currently very disillusioned."

### Oyewu, from Nigeria

"I did not expect students or anybody to pay any attention to my skin color. It is so base. I know I am Black and the other person is white, brown, or a woman, but such is the obvious. To find that African Americans could not be accepted in my college's white fraternity, and I was accepted, did not make sense. I was told later told that I was accepted because I was a foreigner. A Black student had confronted me and asked me why I was in a white fraternity. At first, I was mad at him because I was sick and tired of everybody referring to me by my skin color. I asked him to explain how it mattered. Angrily he stated that, by my being in that fraternity, I was selling out the rest of the Black students. I started to understand the race politics. I moved out of the fraternity to live off campus with my brother, feeling angry. I was angry that the white students treated me with civility which I interpreted as good, and which I questioned later. I was angry at the college administrators that they would encourage such illogical behaviors and attitudes. I stopped going to church although I always pray to God on my own. That incidence helped me to see America for what it is. It is painful that I had to come here to understand colonialism and its injustices to the African people. I am so glad I attend a predominantly white institution, because I now understand that civility is not necessarily genuine."

### Commentary

It is clear from the students' responses about their expectations that their college experiences, especially exposure to racism, have made them critical thinkers. Questions on democracy and how it is subtly undermined by racism bewildered the students, but through the process they became sensitized to other inequalities in their home countries and indeed the world. Respecting figures of authority was not new to these students, and they generally kept away from confronting their professors even when they perceived themselves as correct.

## Personal Relationships and the Social Scene

Students were asked to describe their personal relationships and social life while they attended their predominantly white institutions. Their responses follow.

### Furaha, from rural Tanzania

"I hang with other foreign students whom I met during the college orientation, and we have a lot of fun together. I have had more fun in college than ever before in my life. My parents did not allow me to go out and dance because such outings are considered evil in their faith. Here I decide when to go out and for how long after my school assignments are done. My best friend comes from Mexico, and we take the same courses and we have a lot in common although we come from different countries. Not only is our religion the same, but the thinking of our parents are so similar that we cannot believe our similarities when we share our past experiences. American students keep to themselves, and we do the same, because we have accents that they say they do not understand."

Furaha is the firstborn in her family and is a student in a private Roman Catholic college in Pennsylvania. Her parents, extended family, and friends from her country paid for her college education. She was also in a private Roman Catholic high school in Tanzania.

### Karamshi, from Indonesia

"After one year of loneliness, I decided that isolating myself in my politeness does not pay and nobody pays me any attention. In fact, I realized that in this culture politeness is equated to stupidity. Very different from my culture. I therefore decided to contest for the position of president in my halls, and I was voted in by all students, including the white students who did not speak to me. I loved debate in Indonesia and I prepared my speech well, made it logical and convincing. I was cheered and that transformed me. I have been on dates with girls who even ask me out. It is different here; in Indonesia you take only your girlfriend out. Here a girl can go dancing with you, pay for her drinks, and thank you for a good time and there is no intimacy. I love it."

### Ghai, from India

"I am the president of my engineering club. I have slowly lost my accent and mannerisms like 'I beg your pardon.' Americans used to think I was pretending to be an English chap and I read the discomfort. If somebody said 'thank you,' I would say, 'not at all.' I now say, 'you are welcome.' Eventually, I have found that the more I differ from everyone else, the more uncomfortable the American students would get with me. So to be a part of the group, I am using slang and people laugh. You see I realized that American students, both Black and white, cannot stand people who speak anything else but English. Believe me I have learned the hard way. Now American guys seek me out and even take my opinion seriously. I am also doing very well socially and academically within my department."

### Nina, from Taiwan

"Basically, students here hang on the basis of color or ethnicity. For example, in the student union building, although all students are welcome, various students know their spots. There is one spot for the Asian students, which include students from Korea, Hong Kong, Taiwan, and China. There is a place where the Blacks, Latinos, and Indonesians hang, and another place for the sororities and fraternities and the other white students. American white students from the rural areas are very narrow-minded and are prejudiced because they are not exposed to others who are not like them. White students from urban areas are cool. Black students would reach out to you from the point of view of validating you as another minority, but it soon becomes obvious that there is no other connection. It is a pity to see what discrimination does to the human mind. It oppresses you and makes you identify with others who are labeled like you by the color of their skin. I have never felt like a minority in my life, and I do not feel like one in this culture although there is pressure to label me."

## Mumbi, from Kenya

"My luck started at the orientation. The people I met then have become my support group, and I am glad I attended the college orientation. Oh, man, I cannot stand some American students! They think they are better than you are. I feel like saying there is no love lost between me and the few that treat me negatively, but then I fear I would be behaving like them at the end of the day. I think that my best weapon is to study hard in order to graduate so that I can argue from a point of strength. It is especially true with those so-called professors who are so narrow-minded about human relations that I hide from them in class, in case I argue with them and risk my grades. I just want my certificate, and off I go. I sometimes regret coming here, but then I would not have been as informed about the hypocrisy as I have witnessed. It helps to talk about it with other foreign students, and sticking together has been a blessing in disguise."

## Kabede, from Ethiopia

"The American culture is divided on color lines, and one gets to learn the fact more through the media than in actual fact. One is labeled minority or majority and from there on, the music is on. The label sets the treatment. The urban kids behave quite differently, and you can always tell that those who give trouble are from the rural areas. They are ignorant and narrow-minded, and the foreign students should take it as such and not personally. The attitudes of foreign students must be in the right position."

Kabede reported that one time four drunk white students called him a "camel jockey" and asked him to go back where he belonged. Such behavior, Kabede observed, came more from white students from the rural areas, where they had never seen other people different from their own ethnic group. In most cases, they were not well traveled either, and their curriculum in high school may not have included the study of other cultures.

## Commentary

There is no doubt that as a result of their college experiences, the students developed socialization coping skills, among them communication and the ability to choose the battles worth fighting. Some also became assertive and identified other groups of students as racist. For example, white students who came from rural areas were perceived as less accepting of people different from them, whereas white students from the city were not.

# Success of College Orientation Programs

Students were asked their opinions of how well their orientation programs facilitated their adjustment to college; they were also asked what they wished would have been included in their orientation programs. Their responses follow.

### Mumbi, from Kenya

"Orientation was for me a chance to meet my freshman class. It was also a chance to get to know the important faces in my university: college deans, president, registrar, bursar, and dean of students, each of who spoke about the school culture. Another important person is the academic adviser who will tell you what courses to take and the sequence."

### Ghai, from India

"Somebody should have informed me about the racial divisions. I would not have been as shocked as I was. I do not know what I should have done, but maybe I would have been on guard to avoid myself being caught unawares."

### Oyewu, from Nigeria

"I regret not knowing the truth about racial divisions. To experience it gives a feeling of being cheated. I felt like that at the fraternity. I was reciprocating with genuine appreciation as it is the case in my culture. You cannot be unkind to somebody who is kind to you. Only a wild animal would behave that way."

### Karamshi, from Indonesia

"Somebody should have informed me about the American ignorance about other cultures, peoples, and countries. I would then not have been so mad when all manner of questions were asked of me, my country, and my people."

### Helina, from rural Ethiopia

"Somebody should have informed me about the international student's association. I learned about them during my final year and realized that I had missed out on a lot of activities."

### Aidoo, from Nigeria

"Somebody should have told me the truth about America. I came here filled with the Hollywood and the democratic fantasy."

### Furaha, from rural Tanzania
"Somebody should have told me more about customer relations and credit management. Finance transactions are more key in this culture than mine at home."

### Commentary
Information about racial divisions was key to the students' responses about how orientation programs could have served their needs better. The students' main source of misinformation about the United States was the media and especially the Hollywood industry, which they perceived as painting positive images of Black and white harmony. As a result, students did not expect racism when they came to America. From the interviews it was evident that the students spent time learning American history and geography—and indeed the history and geography of the whole world. They also expected that all Americans would be literate, because most books and magazines that they read in their countries were printed in the United States.

# Advice for Incoming International Students of Color

The students were asked to offer specific advice to incoming international students of color. Their responses follow.

### Nina, from Taiwan
"Racial composition of students should not matter to the student. One should look for the academic opportunities offered by the institution that has meaning to their educational goal. The newcomers should not be shy; it does not matter who they are, if they are shy they suffer more. Students should get involved in organizations and activities early in the semester. They should also enroll in an exercise program to help them release the stress that accumulates with time. They should also buy notes that many companies like Nittany Notes of State College take for most of undergraduate classes. They should pick a good adviser and not hesitate to ask the professors any questions to clarify what they did not understand."

### Mumbi, from Kenya
"The important thing is to get involved in activities outside the class. This will enable you to meet more people and learn about the American way of life and about yourself."

### Ghai, from India

"The American society is divided along color lines, and you get to learn this from the newspaper. So read the newspapers to be informed. Then get involved. Join class activities and, if you live in residence halls, join hall activities. Your attitude as a foreign student should be in the right perspective. If you are negative, you will perceive everything negatively, and that will affect everything you do in or outside of class. Remember that there are trade-offs on getting the education; it is not all rosy—ignorance by some professors about you and your culture are a part of the package, unfortunately. Whether one likes it or not, there is heterogeneity in the package of education. If anybody laughs at your accent, do not take it personally; ask them why they are laughing. If it is a word you pronounce differently, ask them to tell you how it's pronounced in the United States. They are just ignorant and, in that ignorance, find you amusing."

### Oyewu, from Nigeria

"Find out all the academic prerequisite courses like pre-calculus. Read the syllabus so that you can compare with what you may have done in your home country, because you need the competitive edge in addition to the language problem. The American accent is different from the British, and you need to make the connection. When one has academic deficiencies, that is double jeopardy. Look into auditing courses if you feel that the teaching is different from your home country. You do not earn credits auditing, so you have to understand that you will probably graduate one year after, but with better mastery of your field. Many professors will allow a sit-in if you are not sure, so ask. Get involved. Bring artifacts, pictures, and music from home to remind you who you are. Never get carried away by the American Hollywood fantasy and forget why you came to America. Read books about your home country and develop a critical mind. Bring spices from home so that you do not forget home. You must be receptive to new ideas and new ways of life, but not be receptive to new ideas for the sake of ideas. Be critical and willing to adapt to the American culture. Buy motor insurance if you drive a car, and obey the state laws. Should you happen to come to a stop sign and there are no cars coming, you must still stop. American roads are good, and if [you are] attempting to drive fast, be careful. Find a home in a church so that you can establish long-lasting schools out of the classrooms."

### Karamshi, from Indonesia

"Get involved and take courage to approach the American students first, because they would not make the first move. I run for a position in the halls for the academic organization, and that involvement is what helped my college adjustment. If you say 'I will not try because I am a foreigner,' that is not what the Americans think. That is more in your mind than others'. American students do not care; so long as you know what you want to run for and can convince them, they will support you. The foreigner will have to explain himself and pronounce the words the American way to help with the adjustment. Sometimes the Americans are afraid of you because they do not know you. Nature versus nurturance. The way one behaves is more important than the skin color. If you are the foreigner, make the first effort; and you will be surprised how alike the other person is. Usually, it is the mannerisms that determine your success more than skin color."

### Furaha, from rural Tanzania

"Choose smaller colleges where you can get more personal attention, and don't be indecisive about your major for too long, or you will end up with many credits but not enough credits to get any degree."

## Commentary

It seems that the international students learn much from their fellow students. Those observations are very important, and new students need to know that learning goes on concurrently in class and out of class; so involvement in extracurricular activities is as important as studying. It is worth noting that the comments by Mumbi—"The important thing is to get involved in activities outside the class"—came from a student with a 3.91 GPA.

The advice that these students give to others goes well with the popular saying "Our minds control our behaviors." The power of the mind is therefore underscored as an important attribute for students who are making the transition from high school to college. It is the power of the mind that provides one with self-determination to succeed in spite of stumbling blocks like racism and other distractions that might be oppressive to the student.

# Conclusion

As observed at the beginning of this chapter, there are similarities that the interviewed students shared about their college experiences. Most of them indicated that they viewed college as a learning experience not only in making the grades but about life and the world around them. The experiences brought worthwhile changes to their lives, although racial divisions were difficult to deal with at the beginning. Racial tensions were also somewhat of a rude awakening for the students, who realized that the real United States was not the same as that presented by the media and the country's publicized democratic ideals.

It was interesting that, in spite of the students' negative encounters, all of them reported that they would recommend other students to the same predominantly white institution. They would make these recommendations because of the freedom demonstrated in dealing with all issues in the United States, including racial ones. In some cases, the students used their experiences to better understand themselves and the inequalities in their own countries that they were previously unaware of. It was obvious that they had become critical about their environments and realized that Americans are not all alike. This is indicated by their ability to distinguish the rural students' racist behavior from the behavior of students with an urban background. The open way of dealing with issues also sensitized the students over other inequalities, such as economics, sexism, elitism, and the class system. This new awareness posed individual challenges to the students.

Academically, the students were not surprised by the rigors and requirements of college, as was well expressed by their choices of majors, which included medicine, engineering, computer science, law, and journalism. Most important, all of the students interviewed had financial support of parents and other social support which contributed positively to their high academic performances. Education in their home countries required qualification based on stiff competition and is highly valued, due to shortages of institutions of higher learning and the lack of options for specialized study in such fields as computer science. College orientation was considered helpful, and participation by new international students was recommended.

For all of the students interviewed, there was a fierce determination on the part of parents for all the children to succeed in school, even in spite of both the phenomenal official and hidden costs of education to the parents.

# Chapter 12

# Students Discuss
# Their Perceptions of
# Life at PWIs

Marc Levey

$\mathbf{T}$his chapter presents the observations, feelings, and beliefs of sixty-two students attending predominantly white institutions (PWIs), who were interviewed between January 1995 and March 1996. These students represented a very wide cross-section of a student population that was new to post-secondary education.

In this chapter I share some of the key comments and observations of the students interviewed. In their entirety, the interviews are rich in detail and might deserve a book of their own. My intent here is to use the students' own words to convey the essence or spirit of what was said. In many cases, the student interviewees conveyed very strong opinions and emotions. I hope you will feel this in their words.

## Interview Background

The interview group ranged in age from seventeen to forty years old. They identified themselves as African American, Hispanic/Latino, Native American, Pacific Islander, Asian American, European American, white, or biracial/mixed race. Even though racial/ethnic identification was totally optional, all sixty-two participants volunteered such information. Of the sixty-two interviewees, fifty-one identified themselves as belonging to a racial or ethnic minority or as mixed race, while the remaining eleven identified themselves as either white or European American.

The students interviewed for this chapter lived and attended schools across the country, from Massachusetts to Arizona. In addition, several students came to schools in the States directly from their homes in the American Virgin Islands and Puerto Rico.

Six participants were married, and three had dependent children living with them. Over half reported that they worked at least part-time while attending school. A majority of the interviewees attended four-year colleges and universities, but the group also included nineteen students from two-year institutions and proprietary schools.

Forty students were interviewed individually, and twenty-two in small groups of three to five. After the interview, each participant was asked to fill out a questionnaire, a copy of which appears on pages 222–223. Both individual and group interviews were informal and open-ended; that is, they were not limited to a specific set of questions, but rather were allowed to develop and move into areas that seemed most relevant to the participants.

These student interviews do not constitute scientific research, but instead provide a series of detailed snapshots of students' perceptions of their experiences, observations, and beliefs. Most important, they provide some valuable insights into the post-secondary school experience from a wide range of perspectives.

# Interview Highlights

Several important trends about student life emerged from the interviews, and they are summarized as follows:

✔ Students reported that they studied an average of 10 to 15 hours per week in high school, the overall range being 3 to 45 hours per week.

✔ During their first post-secondary semester or quarter, interviewees reported that they studied an average of 28 hours per week, with 8 hours per week being the lowest and 45 hours per week the highest.

✔ The mean GPA (grade-point average) goal of the students was a 3.30 on a 4.00 scale.

✔ More than 80 percent of the interviewees (fifty individuals) reported that they *always* study alone.

✔ A large majority of the interviewees reported that they found the academic work in college to be more demanding than they thought it was going to be.

✔ Developing and maintaining a viable social life appeared to be a serious and widespread problem, especially for female minority interviewees. There seemed to be little difference across race with this problem, with majority students reporting difficulty in this area in about the same proportion as students of color.

✔ For the students of color who participated in these interviews, racial issues seemed to be their primary concern on predominantly white campuses; whereas for white students, academic performance and, more specifically, grades topped their list of concerns.

✔ For more than 80 percent of the interviewees who identified themselves as minorities (forty-one individuals), the decision to attend a PWI appeared to be a positive one at this early point in their academic careers.

# Questionnaire

The following are the questions the interviewer will ask all interviewees. Each interview will take approximately one half-hour.

## Demographics

Name (optional) _____

Phone number (optional) _____

Age _____

Gender _____

Hometown address:   ☐ inner city           ☐ suburbs

☐ small city or town   ☐ rural

Race or ethnic background (optional) _____

Approximate income status of parents:

☐ low (below $20.000 per year)
☐ low middle ($20,000–$40,000 per year)
☐ middle ($40,000–$70,000 per year)
☐ high ($70,000 and up)

## Academics

1. When did you first begin to think about college?
2. How did you gather information?
3. Were your parents involved? How much?
4. Were they supportive?
5. Who in the school, if anybody, was helpful?
6. If you have some notion of what your major should be, how did you arrive at that choice?
7. What kinds of things about academics did you need to know more about before you arrived on campus?
8. What surprised you the most in the classroom? Academics in general?
9. How many hours per week did you study in high school?
10. How many did you expect you would have to study in college?
11. How many hours per week do you actually study?
12. What is your GPA goal?

13. Do you study most often alone or in groups?
14. Do you believe the instructors are better, the same, or worse than in high school?
15. Are your academic performance expectations and your parents' the same?
16. Is there anything else a prospective minority student needs to know about academics, studying, major selection, etc.?

### Personal

1. Why did you choose a PWI?
2. What other institutions did you consider?
3. What did you expect in terms of the living environment?
4. What did you find?
5. What was the hardest thing for you to adjust to?
6. What is the best thing about living here?
7. Describe your social life.
8. Do you date or have close friends across race, national, or ethnic lines? If not, why?
9. What is the chief value for a student of color in attending a PWI?
10. What is the chief drawback?
11. Have you encountered any problems centered on race or ethnic background?
12. Do you believe you have control over your life at this time?
13. If you could change one thing about your present life overnight, what would it be?
14. Looking back, would you have made your decision to attend this institution differently?

### Informed Consent Form

The authors of the book project, *How to Succeed on a Majority Campus: A Guide for Minority Students,* are conducting personal interviews, all or parts of which will form the basis of one chapter. You are asked to share your expectations of college life prior to arriving on campus versus what you actually experienced. By agreeing to participate in these interviews, you are consenting to have any material taped to be used by the authors. Your participation is voluntary and confidential.

Name _____ Date _____

These interviews demonstrate that there is an extremely wide variety of expectations and experiences even within racial or ethnic groups. In other words, it seems to me a mistake to assume that *all* or even *most* Blacks, Hispanics, Asians, or whites will have the same expectations or experiences in college. If these interviews prove nothing else, they show decisively the diversity and individuality within groups. The lesson here is that even if you identify with a certain nationality or racial/ethnic group, you are first and foremost a unique individual.

## Student Perceptions About Academics

In answer to the question of who had been most helpful to them academically, students did not think high school guidance counselors helped them very much. The representative comments that follow reflect this sentiment with force.

*"My guidance counselor didn't seem to want to help me. He was too busy being a hard-ass ... They're all just cracking the whip."*
—Shanna, an inner city African American student

*"A lot of people, but for sure not my counselor. Man, she was a waste!"*
—-Luis, who went to high school in a medium-sized city in the Southwest

*"I had to help myself, because my counselor was only interested in helping the smart kids."*
—A white student

*"My guidance counselor told me that maybe I should go to a tech school, because she didn't think my English made me 'college material.'"*
—-Tran, a Vietnamese student who had been in the United States for about six years

Whether the dozens of other negative comments about guidance counselors are an accurate reflection of the entire system, or whether it's just students blowing off steam, is hard to say. What is clear is that, at least for this group of students, help and information about postsecondary schools did not, with a few notable exceptions, come from established counseling services in the public school system.

### Students' Perceptions of Their Academic Needs

Students were also questioned about the kinds of academic issues they thought it would have been useful to know more about when entering college. This question elicited surprisingly similar responses from a majority of the interviewees. Most would have wanted to know more about just how much work they needed to do, the difficulty of the material, and how good or bad the teachers were. As the quotes that follow demonstrate, for some students this became an emotional issue.

*"I didn't think I'd have to work my butt off the way I do. I did real good in high school without doin' any real work, maybe a couple of hours here and there."*

—A white lower-income student from a small rural community in Pennsylvania

*"I need to struggle to keep my head in the academic game. It's not like high school at all. The profs don't care if you're there or not. It's up to you. I guess I thought someone would see that I went to class or got my homework done. Boy, was I wrong!*

—Karl, a white first-year student at a technical institute

*"I needed to understand how what you took for classes has a lot to do with what you want to do with your life. You just can't take any old thing, like, you gotta' have a plan."*

—Chris, a first-year biracial student from northern New Jersey

*"Even though I knew I was going to a PWI and it would be big, it didn't hit me that I might be alone until I went to my first large class of two hundred, looked around, and didn't see anyone else that looked like me."*

—Reggie, an African American student attending a large midwestern public university

# Student Perceptions of Parental Involvement

The questions I raised in every interview about parental involvement and support in making post-high school educational plans yielded some interesting results. To a large extent, parents were involved in some part of their children's decision making about future schooling. A notable exception to this was among Asian American students, who reported that their parents were far less involved than any other racial or ethnic group.

Questions about support for the decision to attend a particular school and support and encouragement once the students arrived on campus produced mixed results. In both areas parents from all racial/ethnic groups were generally very positive and encouraging. The mixed part of the student responses comes when you look at the differing support of the mother and father. More than 40 percent of the interviewed students under age twenty-five (twenty-two individuals) reported greater involvement, support, and encouragement from their mothers than their fathers, both before beginning school and during the first several months of classes. Several students reported no involvement from their fathers at all, even though both parents resided in the same household.

There seemed to be no significant difference in the level of support of mothers and fathers based on racial/ethnic group, except when it comes to Asian American fathers and their daughters. In these interviews Asian American women reported a good deal less involvement and support from their fathers than interviewees in any other group.

The way students describe their interaction with their parents can be very revealing. Carmen, a first-semester student at a two-year college in Boston, put it this way:

*"My father couldn't care less. He thinks I should quit. Mom's the one who always pushed me in school. Lots of times she and my dad had fights over me because of school."*

Jason, a Native American from Santa Fe, New Mexico, had a different experience:

*"My people didn't know enough about college to help me much, so they left the finding out and decisions to me. Now that I'm in, they're sure happy and tell everybody they know. It makes me feel kinda' good; they're happy, I'm happy."*

A much different perspective is presented by Kim, a nineteen-year-old beginning student attending an art school in Philadelphia:

*"From the very beginning, my father and sometimes my mother tried to talk me out of art school. I don't think they really thought I had any talent. It was only when I wouldn't change my mind that they ... especially my mom started to come around ... I still feel my parents wish I had chosen a different school with fewer 'weirdoes.' It's probably hard for them to tell the rest of the family where I go to school ... what I'm studying."*

A glowing report came from La Ronna, an eighteen-year-old attending a branch campus of a large public university:

*"Nobody in my family ever went to college. They all groove on my going. The first time I went home in the fall, they all asked me all these questions about medicine, politics, and that stuff as if I had all of a sudden become the world's great expert on everything. Kind of okay, but lots of pressure."*

### Parent's Expectations About Academic Performance

In answer to a question concerning students' and parents' academic performance expectations, the interviewees' responses were, not unexpectedly, mixed. There was just about an even split in students who reported similar expectations between their parents and themselves and those who had much different expectations from their parents. Surprisingly, more than 20 percent of the students(fourteen individuals) reported that their parents voiced no academic performance expectations whatsoever. A sample of the responses to this issue follow.

*"My folks support my going to school, but since they didn't go to school they don't know what to expect."*
—Emilio, a first-semester Chicano student pursuing a major in broadcast communications

*"My parents have very high expectations of me since I am the first one to go on to college. They think I should get A's in everything. Jesus, they don't realize the pressure that put on me."*
—Albert, a second-semester white lower-income student attending an elite school on an athletic scholarship

*"I expect too much of myself. It's like if I don't do very well, I'll disappoint my family and their friends."*
—Tommy, a first-generation Korean American student

# Students' Reasons for Attending a PWI

In answer to the question of why students chose to attend a predominantly white institution, there were three basic responses. All had to do with the reputation of PWIs and the perceived benefits that they could eventually bring to the student. One type of response had to do with the special "get-ready" or support programs offered by many PWIs. A second type had to do with the reputation of PWIs compared with historically Black institutions (HBIs). And the third type of response addressed the wide choices that PWIs offered in both the number of schools to choose from and the variety of courses and majors offered by those schools. Some sample responses follow.

*"Even though I really wanted to go to a Black college, my father talked me into applying to BU [Boston University]. To my surprise, I was accepted. I became convinced that BU would do more for me than anyplace else I applied to."*

—Ron, an African American pre-med student at Boston University

*"All the time I wanted to go to a top engineering school, and there just aren't many Black schools that have really good engineering programs, especially nuclear."*

—Aaron, an African American engineering student at a
Big Ten university

*"The only way I could go to school was by being admitted through a special program, and I guess that's better than a community college. Anyway, they gave me money because I'm Hispanic and nobody else offered up as much.... This is the only way I could go to such a good school."*

—Robert, an Educational Opportunity Program student attending a
large state university

*"Isn't it true that almost all really good colleges are mostly white? At least that's what I thought."*

—Linda, a biracial first-semester student at a big city university

*"With all their alumni and stuff, I should get a high-paying job easier when I graduate. The recruiter that came to our high school convinced me on this."*

—Julian, an Asian American student attending one of the largest
schools in the nation

*"Because my grades and SATs were so good, I had my choice of just about any school I wanted. I could have gone to a large state university with a lot of minorities, but I decided to go to a small Ivy League school instead, one, for the education and, two, because I think a degree from here will get me into the architecture grad school at Yale easier."*

—Josie, a first-semester Chinese American student

# Student Perceptions of the Living Environment and Social Life

Questions about student perceptions of their living environments and social life at college revealed some marked differences between what students of color thought they would be like and what they actually turned out to be. To be sure, some students gauged these issues accurately either because a friend or someone in their family had previously attended a PWI, or because they did a lot of research, including campus visits. These students found that college living held no real surprises for them. For the majority of students, however, one or more characteristics of their living environment surprised and, in a few cases, shocked them.

For most minorities interviewed, the sheer number of white students all but overwhelmed them at first. Although most of the minority students reported that they had witnessed racism at some point in their lives, several stated that they experienced racism or segregation directed at them personally for the first time only after arriving on their respective campuses. In relation to their living environment, some students seemed to be most concerned with the effectiveness of their study habits and studying in general, whereas others focused on racial issues and adjustment to a new and sometimes hostile environment. Some representative quotes follow.

*"I expected lots of white faces and that's exactly what I got. But it sure was weird being the only person of color on my dorm floor."*
> —Brian, an African American first-semester student at a large university with a less than 5 percent Black student enrollment

*"My high school was mostly Black and Hispanic. I don't think I was ready for the sea of white. After three months I still don't feel comfortable here. I'm thinking about transferring."*
> —Shellie, a Hispanic/Black woman in her first semester at a medium-sized state college in the East

*"Being verbally assaulted was not what I came here for. I don't need to put up with this crap."*
> —John, a Chinese American student whose family has lived in the United States for more than one hundred years

*"I have been more or less cut off from my old hometown buddies here at school just because a couple of my good [new] friends are Black. My former 'buddies' really suck ... Screw 'em."*

———Angelo, a white athlete from an almost totally white small city in eastern Pennsylvania

*"I found both good and bad just like at home. The difference was that I had to make the choices."*

—Kelvin, an African American first-semester broadcast communications student

*"What I found was a totally different school setup. No force-feeding; in fact, some instructors don't seem to care to know me at all. I went to a prep school where everybody knew everybody. Very different now."*

—Carrie, a Mexican American student from south Texas

*"The American culture was very difficult for me to adjust to. It's so fast-paced."*

—Tia, a female first-semester student from American Samoa

*"I adjusted easily. That's probably because I've spent some weekends here visiting my brother, who's a junior."*

—Jackson, an African American engineering student

*"[The hardest thing about adjusting was] being a minority at a large institution, I mean being a 'real minority.'"*

—Juan, a male Latino student at a large midwestern university

*"The hardest thing for me to adjust to was being independent and taking responsibility for myself. I always had my parents to depend on every day. Now I can afford to talk to them only once a week. This is what growing up is all about, isn't it?"*

—Roxie, an African American scholarship student

*"The pain won't go away. I've never been called 'nigger' to my face before. I know it's wrong to feel this way, but I just want to smash somebody."*

—Carlos, a self-identified Black Puerto Rican theater major

*"I've tried to adjust to all these minorities yelling for equality. What the hell do they want from me? I never owned any slaves."*

—Jason, a white second-semester student from suburban Washington, D.C.

## Social Life

Where minority students differed greatly from their white counterparts was in their focus on their social environment. As one might expect, white students on a predominantly white campus took the social environment in stride—it seemed to them much the same as their previous experiences. These students had the most difficulty in adjusting to a different set of academic expectations and an academic climate that was less forgiving than high school.

For many minority students, however, the adjustment appeared to be far more complex. Most had the same academic adjustment to contend with as did their white student counterparts, and in addition they found themselves having to deal with issues of social climate. One student even quoted the well-known science-fiction writer Robert Heinlein's book title as he struggled to express his feelings about his campus when he described himself as being "a stranger in a strange land." Above all else, many students of color, and in particular Hispanic students, reported that they missed the types of social events like parties and dances they enjoyed in their hometown ethnic neighborhoods.

Descriptions of social life ranged all the way from "It's nonexistent" to "It's all I do." There did not appear to be significant differences between the way whites and minorities described their social lives—with one possible exception: Black and Asian American women reported less active social lives (specifically partying and dating) than any other demographic group. Many of the interviewees, both minority and majority, harbored reservations about the possibility of viable cross-cultural or interracial friendships or dating relationships. On the other hand, about the same number of interviewees, again across race and ethnicity, admitted that these kinds of relationships were possible, even desirable. Only a very small number of students (four), expressed absolute opposition to interracial dating; all of these were women. Numbers of students found that they could and did make friends across racial/ethnic lines. Furthermore, several minority and majority students reported successful intimate dating relationships.

A sample set of responses to questions about the interviewees' perceptions of social life follow.

*"To forget where I am, I party hard every weekend. I can't wait for Friday night."*
    —Ellis, a white second-semester fraternity member

*"I expected nice large rooms and quiet times to study in the dorms. Ho, ho—no way!"*
—Sally, a Latina second-semester student from Puerto Rico

*"The parties got in the way of studying, so I had to make a choice. Study more and survive, or party and go down with a smile on my stupid face."*
—Jacqueline, an African American pre-law student

*"Hispanic parties are a kinda' sanctuary for me. I hear the music and I'm home again. Without them I would have a hard time making it through the week."*
—Mildred, a Latina student from the West Coast

*"I'm too busy with schoolwork to have much of a social life. Anything I do is with my girlfriends."*
—Joan, an Asian American first-year student

*"I've got lots of friends from all races. That's what's so neat about being at a large university in the city."*
—Brian, a mixed-race student from a rural high school in Ohio

*"I've got no social life—none at all. All the Black guys want to go out with white girls. I'm pissed just thinking about it."*
—Jennifer, an African American second-semester student

*"This place is so isolated. There are only thirty-five Blacks. I swore I'd never date a white guy, but what choice did I have? I can't go home every week-end. Anyhow, I met Brian (who's white) and we had so much in common it was as if color didn't matter anymore. Still, I can't take him to West Philly, and he can't take me home with him to Scranton. That tells it all, huh?"*
—Alisha, a second-semester African American student who attends a small satellite campus of a large public university

*"If there are no Hispanic events, I sometimes go out with my non-Hispanic friends. Otherwise, I just stay at home and watch TV."*
—Juan, a Hispanic student in civil engineering

*"This place sucks. No social life, no beer, no nothin' unless you're in a fraternity."*
—Tom, a white student who transferred from a large city college to a small technical institute

*"I got peace to study and lots of parties. Both great!"*
—Joe, a Native American adult student from the Southwest

Participating in or attending ethnic-specific activities such as this step dance can give minority students some sense of identity and history, even at a PWI.

*"One of the most exciting things for me here is the possibility of meeting and maybe dating someone from another race ... perhaps from another country. That's why I came to college—to find out who I am by experiencing other people."*
                    —Edna, a new African American psychology student at a
                                        mid-sized private college

## Positive Perceptions About College

One question posed to students who were new to post-secondary education asked them to comment on their positive perceptions of life on campus. In the main, the positive experiences revolved around meeting new and interesting people as well as having a feeling of independence.

*"The best thing about living here on campus is the new friends I've been able to meet. I was sort of shy in high school and I'm just coming out of it now."*
                    —Maria, a second-semester student from the Bronx

Numbers of students report that they found "community" by joining histori-cally black Greek organizations. More and more race-specific fraternities and sororities are springing up at PWIs all across the country.

*"I've been able to meet lots of people from different races and backgrounds. It's opened me up to new possibilities."*
—Lori, a first-semester white student from Philadelphia

*"Being on my own and making my own decisions for a change is a rush. I could never go back to living in my parents' house again."*
—Connstance, a Taiwanese American student from New England

*"Living in a mostly white dorm has made me appreciate my culture more. It also makes me miss my music and food a lot more than I thought I would."*
—Raymond, a Hispanic student from Providence, Rhode Island

*"I think what I gain from living in a white society is that it will get me ready for the world of work. I have to be multicultural myself."*
—Charelle, an African American student with an international business major

*"Living here draws you closer to your culture. I try to teach other people about Black history."*
—William, a newly naturalized adult student originally from Nigeria

# Advice for Other Minority Students

Toward the end of each interview session, I asked the interviewees to share advice for prospective or beginning minority students who had decided to attend a predominantly white institution. What follows are several of the most thoughtful responses.

*"Freedom initials responsibility."*

*"Be what you want to be, not what you think others want you to be."*

*"You need to satisfy yourself first."*

*"You can only change yourself; you can't change others."*

*"Resist the pressure to fall in with the 'non-study partier,' who will tell you that studying is not cool."*

*"Parents—try not to live through your college kids."*

*"All your actions have consequences."*

*"All relationships are individual, and love is color blind."*

*"Trust your instincts about people."*

*"For some, diversity translates into 'them' and 'us.'"*

*"Diversity means tolerating people you shouldn't have to tolerate."*

*"Sometimes a PWI pushes you away from your culture and to the dominant one."*

*"Open heart, cautious mind."*

# Conclusion

After these interviews and more than twenty-five years of experience working directly with students of color at a predominantly white institution, I am certain of one thing: There is a trap set for all of us in making any generalized assumptions about a group of people whose common identifier is skin color or national origin. Stereotypes are born out of ignorance, and ignorance is a product of lack of contact. I've also found out that for both whites and students of color, the more extensive their contact with one another, the more likely it is that racial hostility and perceptions of threat will diminish.

Again, and I can't repeat this too often, every person brings something unique to a relationship. To assume anything about an entire race or culture is simply self-defeating. There is just no such thing as homogeneity within a race, religion, or culture.

Many authors write about their experiences with minority students and describe stereotypic behavior. However, what should be obvious by now is that it is up to you alone to determine with what groups you choose to identify, and what type of individual—amidst all the stereotypes, generalizations, and categorizations that others will apply to you—you are striving to be.

## DATE DUE

| | | | |
|---|---|---|---|
| | | | |
| | MAR 1 2 1998 | | |
| | | | |
| | | | |
| | | | |
| | | | |
| | | | |
| | | | |
| | | | |
| | | | |
| | | | |
| GAYLORD | | | PRINTED IN U.S.A. |